HAUN
ENFIELD

HAUNTED
ENFIELD

Jason Hollis

The
History
Press

Dedicated to Katherine and Paul

First published 2013

The History Press
The Mill, Brimscombe Port
Stroud, Gloucestershire, GL5 2QG
www.thehistorypress.co.uk

© Jason Hollis, 2013

The right of Jason Hollis to be identified as the Author
of this work has been asserted in accordance with the
Copyright, Designs and Patents Act 1988.

British Library Cataloguing in Publication Data.
A catalogue record for this book is available from the British Library.

ISBN 978 0 7524 9312 1

Typesetting and origination by The History Press
Printed and bound by TJ International Ltd, Padstow, Cornwall

CONTENTS

ACKNOWLEDGEMENTS

I owe a debt of gratitude to many people for their assistance and support. Most notably, I would like to thank my wife Emma, my parents, Janet Thompson and her family, Graham Dalling, Kate Godfrey, Steve Dowbiggin OBE, Bryan Hewitt, Terry Oliver, Sarah Scales, Peter Everett, Martin Harrow, Jane Hodgson, Alex Mattingly, David Farrant, Celia Gooch, Gavin Williams, Vicky Sanderson, Maria Hamer, Oliver and Adam of Trent Park Open House, Christine Matthews, Leonard Will, Justin Hobson – and of course Mickey, Louise and the rest of the NLPI team.

© Jay Hollis, 2006

INTRODUCTION

I have had a fascination with ghosts since childhood and have collected many books on true hauntings. The books concerning London usually include a couple of entries for Enfield, but always the same ones. I was born in Enfield and lived there for many

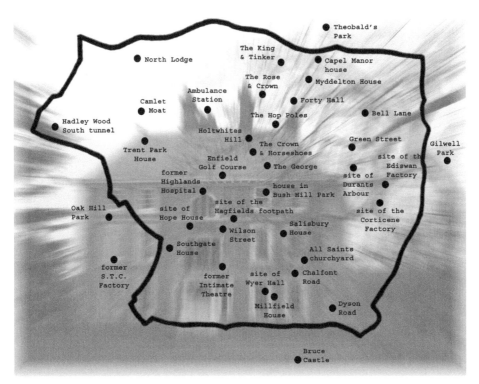

Haunted places in and around the London Borough of Enfield. (© Jay Hollis, 2013)

years before moving to Hertfordshire, and it always disappointed me that other haunted locations within the borough were never mentioned. To end my disappointment, I decided to write this book.

I started my research in 2000, never thinking that it would take thirteen years to complete the book. That's not to say I have been writing it for thirteen years. I gave up a number of times and life had a habit of taking precedence: since then I have met, courted and married my lovely wife, faced the uncertainty of redundancy and re-employment and become a father to two wonderful children, who are a constant distraction.

Perhaps it was inevitable, but after almost twelve years of researching ghosts I joined North London Paranormal Investigations (NLPI) and I am now one of their key investigators. Having been with them for a year I still class myself as a novice in the field and, as most of this book was written before I had even considered becoming a paranormal investigator, it should not be read as the memoirs of a 'ghost hunter'. Indeed, it is not that, but rather a collection of stories that have been gathered together in one volume for the very first time.

I have discovered more haunted sites within the borough than I initially thought existed, although there are probably others yet to be unearthed (and I have deliberately left out a few). However, I am not trying to suggest that Enfield is the 'ghost capital' of the world, or even London, for I believe that if you dig deep enough into the history of an area you'll find plenty of ghosts.

I hope you enjoy this journey through Enfield's shadows. If you have an Enfield ghost story you would like to share, please email me at ghosts@jayhollis.plus.com.

Jason Hollis,
March 2013

1

THE PHANTOM COACH

There are many tales of ghostly horse-drawn coaches from all around the country and they are often embellished with grisly details. Anne Boleyn's coach, for instance, is said to arrive at Blickling Hall in Norfolk, driven by a headless coachman and drawn by headless horses, as is the coach that arrives at Bradgate Park in Leicestershire, carrying the ghost of the equally unfortunate Lady Jane Grey. It would seem that neither of these ladies are about to let anyone forget how they died. Less gruesome, but equally frightening, is the phantom coach and horses that has been seen in the eastern regions of Enfield, most famously in Bell Lane, Enfield Wash, in 1961. However, the first of the various sightings related here occurred a few weeks before Christmas in 1899.

It was a cold, clear, starlit night and sixteen-year-old Mary Read was walking home with two friends, Florence Beatty and Daisy Taylor, from the Edison Swan United Electric Light Co. factory (known to employees as 'The Lamp') in Ponders End, where they were employed in the production of electric light holders. They had been working late and it was dark as they made their way home along a path that crossed the fields to the north of Nag's Head Road; an area that has long since been lost to housing developments.

All of a sudden, a black old-fashioned coach drawn by four horses appeared to rise up from the ground ahead of them, and the three startled girls watched the coach as it careered northwards, towards Brimsdown. They could clearly see a driver sitting at the front and there appeared to be a man leaning out of the window of the carriage as it rocked from side to side. The girls were a little uneasy and unsure of what it was they were witnessing, but what happened next left them with little doubt. The coach had almost reached Durants Arbour, an old and crumbling moated farmhouse, when it suddenly vanished. Mary and her two friends didn't wait to see if the coach would reappear: they ran the rest of the way to a house in nearby Durants Road, where one of them lived.

This manifestation occurred in Ponders End, but most of the reported sightings of the phantom coach have been in Bell Lane, over a mile further north in Enfield Wash. Nineteenth-century Ordnance Survey maps of the area show that Bell Lane used to follow a route that consisted of three long sections, joined together by two short ninety-degree dog-legs. The road ran eastwards away from its intersection with Hertford Road, the main thoroughfare that once formed part of the old road from London to Cambridge. The first of these sections no longer exists, and Bell Lane is now connected to the main road via Eastfield Road. However, there may once have been a relatively straight track that passed through the area, sharing part of its route with what is now Eastfield Road, continuing into Bell Lane; the course that the Phantom coach has been seen to follow suggests that this may be the case, for it was seen here in 1912 by a lamplighter who watched it pass through a house whilst on his round in the early hours of the morning.

In his book *Dark Journey*, paranormal investigator David Farrant relates the testimonies of a number of people, interviewed by him, who had seen the phantom coach. The first of these, chronologically, was David Hanchett, who saw the coach during the Second World War. On the night of 28 June 1944, at about ten o'clock, he was cycling home along Bell Lane. Approaching the junction with Eastfield Road, he noticed two lights on the other side of a hedge bordering some allotments. They were approaching from the south-west (so at this point it was not following the course of either Bell Lane or Eastfield Road) and he stopped to watch as the lights got closer.

His intrigue turned to shock as a ghostly coach drawn by a team of four phantom horses suddenly burst through the hedge and continued to speed along the lane, rocking from side to side, before disappearing through a gate that led to some old garages, which have since been demolished. Mr Hanchett described the carriage as being a tall, black, box-like shape. It was silent, making no sound whatsoever, and an eerie, electric-blue light outlined the entire apparition. It was driven by a coachman in a tall black hat with a long whip at his side, and people could be seen inside the coach as it passed directly in front of him. He also noticed that the wheels were about 1ft off the ground. The same apparition was also seen by a young boy, who ran away in terror.

Another witness interviewed by Farrant was a woman who had lived at Eastfield Cottages in Eastfield Road throughout her childhood. In the early hours of Christmas Day 1957, when she was nine years old, she woke up and looked out of her bedroom window, whereupon she saw a black coach drawn by a team of horses. Thinking that it must be Father Christmas's sleigh laden with presents, she quickly woke up her younger brother and they both watched the coach as it silently passed the gates of Albany Park opposite and disappeared down Bell Lane.

The coach was seen again four years later, about a mile south-west of Bell Lane. Jeanne Ballard was living with her parents in their house on the Great Cambridge Road, the garden of which backed on to the Carterhatch School playing field. As her bedroom was in the process of being redecorated, she was temporarily sleeping on a mattress in

Bell Lane, looking west. (© Jay Hollis, 2012)

the downstairs living room. Sometime after midnight on 4 October 1961 she switched off the light and climbed into her makeshift bed. Suddenly, she heard a loud noise coming from the back of the house. As the sound got louder, she realised it was the sound of horses' hooves. She was just about to get up and investigate when, as Jeanne later described to the local press, 'Suddenly the room was lit up by shafts of light and from behind me, through the rear wall, came a black shiny coach drawn by two pairs of magnificent horses.'

In her interview with the *Enfield Gazette & Observer* Jeanne described seeing two women inside the coach. They were wearing large hats and period dress, and were talking to each other in a very excited manner. She remembered that one of the women was wearing an emerald green dress and that both had very refined accents, and although Jeanne could hear their conversation distinctly, she could not remember anything that they had actually said. She also noticed that part of the coach seemed to be passing through the wall to her right and that the wheels were 2ft off the floor. The coach then veered to the left and disappeared through the wall at the other end of the room.

The most famous encounter with the coach occurred a month later, again on Bell Lane, at around seven o'clock in the evening on Halloween. It was a cloudless and starlit night, very much like the night on which Mary Read and her friends had seen the apparition sixty-two years earlier, and seventeen-year-old Robert Bird

Bell Lane looking east. (© Jay Hollis, 2012)

was cycling westwards along Bell Lane. He had almost reached Albany School, where the lane bends to the right at the junction with Eastfield Road, when he saw two lights ahead of him, about 6ft above the ground and several feet apart. As Robert got nearer he could see that there were two figures sitting between the lights – and that whatever it was, was heading straight for him.

The mysterious object got closer still and Robert could now see another figure, sitting further back. Two pairs of horses began to materialise in front of the lights. They were almost on top of him, and he could now clearly see the coach itself. Terrified, and with no time to get out of the way, Robert braced himself for the inevitable impact as the two leading horses galloped either side of him. He must have felt a sense of both horror

and relief when the entire apparition passed straight through him! As the phantom coach passed around him, he also saw two ladies seated inside the carriage, just as Jeanne Ballard had done … and then it was gone. Hardly able to believe what had just happened, he turned around to find the road behind him empty and silent – the coach and horses had vanished even more quickly than it had appeared.

Robert's frightening experience made the front page of the 24 November edition of the *Enfield Gazette & Observer*. After reading the article, both Jeanne Ballard and Mary Read, now (in 1961) married and in her seventies, contacted the newspaper and their stories were also printed the following week.

No one has yet been able to offer any explanation as to why a phantom coach and horses should be seen in the

Durants Arbour shortly before it was demolished. (© Enfield Local Studies & Archive)

area, and there are no known records of an accident, or any other significant incident involving a horse-drawn coach in Enfield's history. Indeed, there are a number of questions raised by these sightings that may never be answered: Where was the coach going, and where had it come from? Who was inside it? Could there even be more than one coach? The cases related here have the coach seen in different locations and heading in different directions. Robert Bird said it was heading east along Bell Lane, towards the marshes of the Lea Valley, where it is possible that a coach may long ago have come to grief. Indeed, all the sightings on Bell Lane have placed the coach travelling in the same easterly direction, although when David Hanchett first saw the apparition it was coming towards him from the south-

west. However, the coach seen by Jeanne Ballard was travelling westwards, in the opposite direction to the Bell Lane sightings, and the one seen by Mary Read and her friends was heading in yet another direction and appeared to end its journey at Durants Arbour.

Perhaps there is an event in the history of that house to explain the haunting and even identify the occupants of the coach. The old farmhouse that Mary Read would have known as 'The Old Moat House' was built in the eighteenth century on the site of a medieval manor house. Both the farmhouse and its predecessor were surrounded by a moat that existed until 1910, when the building was demolished and the moat filled in to make way for a housing estate. It was once believed, mistakenly, that Durants Arbour had belonged to Judge George

Jeffries (1644-1689), the notorious seventeenth-century 'Hanging Judge' who had hundreds of people executed, often without trial, for supporting the Duke of Monmouth's rebellion against James II. However, it was actually Jeffries' daughter that lived at Durants Arbour rather than the judge himself who, it is believed, may have lived for a time at Salisbury House in Bury Street (see chapter seven).

In Ponders End, after Mary Read and her friends had seen the coach, local rumour said that the occupants of the phantom coach were two queens. There are no historical records to either support or disprove this, but it is nevertheless interesting to note that Jeanne Ballard described two very refined ladies sitting in the coach as it passed through her parents' house.

In Forty Hill, about a mile and a half west of Bell Lane, there is a local tradition that the coach is seen rumbling along a private road that leads to the seventeenth-century Dower House. Are the occupants of the coach connected in some way to that house? It is said to emerge from this narrow, gravelled lane before proceeding eastwards down Goat Lane. It should perhaps be noted that Goat Lane becomes Hoe Lane at the point where it crosses the New River and Hoe Lane continues, despite now being bisected by the A10 dual carriageway, until it meets the Hertford Road, almost opposite its junction with Eastfield Road. It seems likely that these roads may have once formed a single road, and it has been suggested that Bell Lane may be part of an old coaching route that forded the river Lea and continued across Essex all the way to Colchester, although old maps of the area show that the main eastbound coach road crossed the River Lea further south.

The phantom coach is often referred to as 'The Enfield Flyer' or 'Bell Lane Flyer' because of the mistaken belief that the coach travels along Bell Lane 6ft above the ground. If this is the case it could not possibly have passed through Robert Bird in 1961 – unless of course Robert was a 7ft giant riding a penny-farthing bicycle! This is an error that seems to have crept into the story from Robert's own remark in his original interview with the *Enfield Gazette & Observer* that the coaches' lamps, which were the first things he saw, were 'about six foot above the ground'. This would indicate that the coach itself was either 'on' the ground or certainly no more than 2ft above – which would tally with the accounts given by Jeanne Ballard and David Hanchett, who both stated that the coach was about 1ft above the ground. So yes, the 'Enfield Flyer' may well appear to travel above the ground, especially along roads such as Bell Lane which would probably have once crossed the marshlands of the Lea Valley on raised embankments. However, for it to now be seen 'flying' 6ft above the ground is perhaps a little far-fetched – even for a ghost story!

2

THE GREY LADY OF TRENT PARK

Trent Park mansion is almost a mile to the north of Oakwood tube station, surrounded by parkland that once formed part of Enfield Chase. This was an extensive area of land that had been designated as a royal hunting ground from the twelfth century until after the English Civil War in the seventeenth century, when it was given over as common land.

Enfield Chase remained common land until 1777, when George III had the area enclosed and divided. He granted some of the land to his physician, Dr Richard Jebb, as a reward for saving the life of his younger brother, the Duke of Gloucester, at Trento in Austria earlier that year. The following year, Jebb built a small villa on Noddingswell Hill and called it Trent Place, at the King's insistence. However, it is doubtful that the Duke, who seems to have been a chronic hypochondriac, was actually dying. He probably would have recovered without the treatments of Dr Jebb, whose remedies and methods were at best bizarre and at worst hazardous to health. With such a reputation, it is perhaps more surprising that the Duke did not die!

After his death in 1787, Trent Place was bought by the Earl of Cholmondley who sold it to John Wigston of Millfield House in Edmonton. He enlarged Jebb's modest villa, which was sold again in 1813 to John Cumming, who spent around £20,000 on further structural improvements – a considerable amount of money at the time – adding two wings, an attic and cellars. Trent Park, as it was now known, was bought in 1833 by David Bevan, who gave it to his son Robert Cooper Lee Bevan, one of the founders of Barclay's Bank. Both the house and family business passed to *his* son Francis in 1893.

The house was given yet another extensive remodelling between 1926 and 1931 by Sir Philip Sassoon. He had the levels of the first and second floors raised and clad the house with eighteenth-century bricks and stonework from the recently demolished Devonshire House, which had stood in Piccadilly. He also imported a wooden staircase from the same residence and a portico from Chesterfield House, and had specially commissioned murals painted

Trent Place. (Image supplied by The Enfield Society)

inside the building by Rex Whistler that can still be seen today.

Trent Park was acquired by Edward Sassoon in 1908 and inherited by his son, Philip, four years later. Sir Philip Sassoon was, like his father before him, the MP for Hythe in Kent and was said to be the wealthiest man in the country. He was also the First Commissioner of Works and the Under-Secretary of State for Air. He held extravagant parties at Trent Park every weekend from May to August during the 1920s and '30s, and his guestlists read like extracts from the 'who's who' of the period; from royalty and high-ranking politicians such as Edward VIII and Wallis Simpson, Winston Churchill, Anthony Eden and Stanley Baldwin to Hollywood stars such as Charlie Chaplin, Douglas Fairbanks Jnr and Boris Karloff, who as a child had attended Enfield Grammar School.

There are many stories to attest to Sir Philip Sassoon's extravagance. He had a fleet of ten Rolls Royce cars, a private airfield in the grounds with a hangar for his aircraft, and he had a network of tunnels constructed under the house and stable block so that his guests would never see the lower servants; any servant that broke this strict rule of invisibility could face instant dismissal. On the upper lake he kept a variety of exotic aquatic birds such as pelicans, pink flamingos and even king penguins which he liked to feed himself. He died of a lung infection in 1939.

During the Second World War the house was used as a prisoner-of-war camp and interrogation centre for high-ranking Luftwaffe officers. There were concealed microphones installed in many of the rooms and a team of surveillance officers would listen in to the conversations that took place between the inmates after they had been 'officially' interrogated, thus revealing many secrets vital to the war effort. After the war, Trent Park became

Sir Philip Sassoon's redesigned house. (Image supplied by The Enfield Society)

a teacher training college and for many years, until 2012, it was the headquarters of Middlesex University.

With such a history, one would assume that Trent Park is haunted by the crackpot Dr Jebb, the flamboyant Philip Sassoon, or perhaps even a German officer who has yet to return to his homeland. However, Trent Park's ghost is that of a Grey Lady, in nineteenth-century crinolines, who was seen by members of the university staff, always accompanied by the smell of lavender. Nobody knows who she is, or was, although a search through nineteenth-century obituaries reveals a couple of possible candidates: John Cumming's wife Eleanor died at Trent Park in 1828 aged fifty-nine, and Lady Elizabeth Agnetha Bevan died in 1851. She was the first wife of Robert Cooper Lee Bevan and her sudden, unexpected death at the age of forty was attributed to a 'spasm of the heart'. Both of these women loved their family home,

so perhaps it is one of them who continues to visit the house after death.

With the exception of the servant's wing, the first- and second-floor levels were raised by about 4ft, as part of Sassoon's redesign of the house. Despite this, the Grey Lady continues to walk along the old levels that she would have known in life – to startling effect. She was once seen simultaneously by two people, one of whom saw her from the waist up, through the floor, while the other, on the floor below, saw only the lower part of her dress seemingly suspended from the ceiling. She has been seen on a number of occasions looking out from a second-storey window, but only ever when the window is open, and the principal's secretary was once somewhat unnerved to see the phantom lady standing in a photocopier.

In 2000, Trent Park's head of security described in an interview with the *Enfield Gazette* how he and a colleague had heard the rustling sound of a crinoline dress coming down the stairs accompanied by the smell of perfume and a sudden, extreme drop in temperature: 'It felt cold – very cold. I didn't like it at all. I'll never go there at night alone again.'

However, he had an even more frightening encounter with Trent Park's ghost one evening when he was locking up. He was at the end of the basement corridor and was just about to lock up a room which, during the 1950s, had been known to the students as 'Mrs Barnet's Tuck Shop', when the door suddenly flew open to reveal the Grey Lady. As if this wasn't frightening enough, he was then chased down the corridor by a mattress!

On another occasion some security guards had a dummy, used by the drama students, thrown at them by an unseen assailant. Perhaps the Grey Lady has a problem with authority figures, or was this the work of a different earthbound soul? For it would seem that the Grey Lady is not alone. Other security guards and members of the university staff have reported seeing figures that have vanished instantly before their eyes.

Sceptics may say that such stories are too bizarre to be believable, but then don't they always? I visited the house on an open day in September 2000 and the guide who showed me around the basement described the head of security as a big man, not easily scared or given to flights of fantasy. This same man had refused to return to the basement alone ever since his encounter there and I certainly wouldn't like to come face to face with something that could unnerve such a man.

But then, I have seen her for myself – or rather, I have seen a photograph taken by *Country Life* magazine in 1908 that some believe shows her ghostly form. It is of the south front as it looked prior to Sassoon's redesigns, and in front of the building is the faint but unmistakeable outline of a woman in a hat and long dress. When I first saw a copy of the photograph I thought that it must have been faked; however, on a second visit to the house in 2012 I was shown a larger, more detailed print of the same photograph by Ken Fisher, who used to work at Trent Park and helps to maintain an archive of material concerning the house and its history. He told me that, some years ago, he gave the photograph to the experts in Middlesex University's photographic department and they conducted various tests but could not find any evidence of tampering. However, it struck me that nobody had examined the original negative and I contacted *Country Life* to see if they could shed some light on the origins of the photograph. They told me that it was *Country Life* policy to remove any people from exterior architectural photographs, and confirmed that the original glass plate negative was now kept at the National Archives in Swindon, which is administered by English Heritage. I have now spoken to them and can confirm that the original glass plate negative was carefully scratched in an effort to remove the female figure from the foreground – it does not show a ghost.

Middlesex University vacated Trent Park in 2012 and, at the time of writing, the future of the house is uncertain. A small group of volunteers held a number of 'Open House Weekends' throughout the summer of 2012, but whether they will be allowed to hold more now depends on whoever

Trent Park in 1903, published by Country Life. *(© Copyright IPC Media Ltd)*

buys the house. It will be a shame if the house remains closed to the public, as it has a fascinating and important history that deserves to be more widely known. Trent Park is worth a visit not just for the house but also for the surrounding parkland, which, unlike the house, is always open to the general public. At the northern tip of the park is an area that is reputed to be haunted by a twelfth-century baron, the subject of the next chapter...

3

CAMELOT'S GHOSTLY RED KNIGHT

To the north of Trent Park, in a tranquil area of dense woodland by Hadley Road, is the site of a moated, medieval manor house called Camlet Moat. The building itself was demolished long ago but the water-filled moat survives and is freely accessible to the public. Very little is known about the place. It has been identified as the possible site of one of the castles of Geoffrey de Mandeville, the twelfth-century Earl of Essex, although that seems unlikely, as he had another castle not far away at South Mimms. What is known is that, according to a fifteenth-century document, 'Camelot Manor' was demolished and the bricks sold to pay for repairs to Hertford Castle in 1440.

Camlet Moat has been excavated twice. First, during the nineteenth century, by Emma Frances Bevan, the second wife of Robert Cooper Lee Bevan, and then again in 1923 by Sir Philip Sassoon. Although Sassoon's efforts were more professional than those of Mrs Bevan, both digs were very amateur affairs and not carried out to the high standard expected of modern

archaeology. As a result, many of the artefacts found have since been lost and there are few records that accurately describe them. Sassoon's excavation revealed that the walls were, in places, 5ft in thickness and the remains of two oak drawbridges were also discovered. So it would seem that 'Camelot Manor' was a fairly substantial and impressive fortification in its heyday. Other finds, such as fourth-century coins, suggest that the site may have seen Roman habitation.

There are a number of legends and traditions associated with Camlet Moat. A well on the site is considered by some to be sacred and an old legend says that the gates of Camlet Moat were so large you could hear them being slammed shut in Winchmore Hill, three miles away. Another legend says that the area is haunted by the ghost of Geoffrey de Mandeville. The story goes that when King Stephen outlawed Geoffrey for treason, he hid his treasure at the bottom of the well at Camlet Moat, then climbed a tree to hide from the King's men. However, he fell from the tree and

Camlet Moat. (© Emma Hollis, 2013)

plunged head-first into the well, where he drowned. His ghost now lurks among the trees, dressed in shining armour and a scarlet cloak, watching any passers-by with intense suspicion.

However, there is enough information about the real man to know that most of this story is nothing but fantasy. Geoffrey de Mandeville was a Norman nobleman whose grandfather, also called Geoffrey, had fought with William the Conqueror at the Battle of Hastings. He was a major player during the early years of the civil war fought from 1139 to 1153, between the rival claimants to the English throne; Matilda, the daughter of Henry I, and her cousin Stephen, who had seized the crown upon Henry's death. During this period both Stephen and Matilda were desperate to maintain the support of the barons who could in turn exploit the situation for their own means. Geoffrey, who initially sup-ported King Stephen, is known to have changed his allegiance at least three times and, in line with the legend, in 1143 the King did indeed declare Geoffrey to be a traitor and stripped him of his lands and titles. Geoffrey fled to the East Anglian fens from where he operated as a 'robber baron', attacking and ravaging the surrounding countryside, and plundering towns, churches and monasteries across East Anglia. These actions resulted in famine for the local people as no crops could be grown during Geoffrey's reign of terror. The Bishop of Winchester, the King's brother, had Geoffrey excommunicated from the church. In August 1144 he was hit in the head by an arrow while besieging one of Stephen's strongholds at Burwell Castle, in Cambridgeshire. Mortally wounded, he was taken to nearby Mildenhall in Suffolk where he died. His body was later buried by the Knights Templar at

Temple church in Fleet Street, London, which indicates that he was perhaps a Templar himself.

Some people have tried to suggest a genuine connection between Camlet Moat and King Arthur. However, King Arthur's legendary castle was first referred to as 'Camelot' by the French writer Chrétien de Troyes, in the latter half of the twelfth century – over 600 years after the real Arthur is supposed to have lived. He also introduced the character of Sir Lancelot into the story and changed the name of Arthur's queen to Guinevere. It is far more likely that 'Camelot Manor' was named with an intention to mirror the Arthurian romance.

Yet another legend connected with Camlet Moat, one that might be true, is that the site was one of the many hideouts used by the highwayman Dick Turpin, who was very active during the 1730s in the countryside north of London, including Enfield. From a secluded vantage point at Camlet Moat he could easily waylay and rob coaches on the old Enfield to Barnet Road (now Hadley Road). So perhaps the cloaked figure that watches people suspiciously from the woodland shadows is not the ghost of de Mandeville at all, but Dick Turpin.

Meanwhile, Geoffrey de Mandeville's ghost is also said to haunt various sites in East Barnet, across the border from Enfield. His appearances were reported by the local newspapers in the 1920s and '30s, prompting several ghost hunts in the East Barnet area. It was claimed that his ghost, clad in shining armour and billowing red cloak, was seen in December 1926 and again on 17 December 1932 in Oak Hill Park by members of the East Barnet Psychical Research Society (EBPRS).

The following week, on Christmas Eve, over 700 people gathered in response to the Society's report in the *Barnet Press* to join the hunt for his ghost! Not everyone had the fortune (or misfortune) of seeing the restless baron, but a few members of the aforementioned society claimed to have also seen him on this occasion.

It was at this time that the EBPRS announced that Geoffrey's ghost appears every six years. However, in 1943 a man who had recently moved into the East Barnet area and claimed to have had no previous knowledge of the legend saw the phantom knight twice, shortly before Christmas. He was seen again in 1946 by local butcher and councillor Eli Frusher. Both these sightings contradict the six-year theory. In fact it seems that Geoffrey de Mandeville has not made an appearance since 1946. The full story of Geoffrey de Mandeville's hauntings in East Barnet and other ghosts

Oak Hill Park, East Barnet. (© Emma Hollis, 2013)

in the area, which is not within the London Borough of Enfield, is told by Jennie Lee Cobban in her book *Geoffrey de Mandeville and London's Camelot*, which I can highly recommend.

Given that de Mandeville died in Suffolk and the story of his hidden treasure is rooted in folklore rather than fact, I am rather sceptical that it is *his* ghost that haunts Camlet Moat and the other locations in East Barnet where he is supposed to have been seen. However, there is a significant event in the history of the area that may suggest an alternate and perhaps more likely identity for the phantom knight, and it surprises me that this has previously been missed.

The Battle of Barnet was fought in the first few hours of daylight on Easter Sunday, 14 April 1471, between the Yorkist army of Edward IV and the Lancastrian supporters of the deposed Henry VI, led by the Earl of Warwick. It was a confused affair, fought in thick fog over a wide area to the north of the town that included the western edge of Enfield Chase. The Lancastrian right flank, under the command of the Earl of Oxford, pushed the Yorkist left flank all the way back into Barnet town but this initial Lancastrian success was not apparent to the rest of the combatants in the thick fog. Consequently, when they returned to the field of battle from the same direction as the Yorkist position, Oxford's men were fired upon by their allies, under the Marquess of Montagu (Warwick's brother) who mistook them for Edward IV's reserves. Some of

Oxford's men fled the field with a cry of treason while others fought back against their attackers. Montagu's men now believed that Oxford had changed allegiance and launched a merciless attack in retaliation. The cry of treason went up all over the field and, in the confusion that followed, Montagu was killed.

Warwick saw his brother fall and, with two-thirds of his own side fighting each other, he knew the battle was lost. Sensing victory, Edward launched all his reserve forces against Warwick, who was pulled from his horse and killed as he attempted to retreat. The Lancastrian army fled the field in any direction they could, but were pursued through the forests, villages and towns that surrounded the area, many being cut down from behind as they ran.

It is certainly plausible that one or more of the fleeing Lancastrian knights may have been killed near Camlet Moat to the east of the battle site or in the areas now known as Oak Hill Park and East Barnet to the south. Perhaps some of them sought refuge and were put to death among the ruins of 'Camelot Manor', which had been demolished thirty years earlier. This is, of course, mere speculation but wherever it happened, many of the fleeing Lancastrians died believing they had been betrayed and their final, desperate, panic-stricken moments may have left a psychic imprint on the area where they fell. I believe that any phantom knights seen in these areas are more likely to be a ghostly reminder of the aftermath of the Battle of Barnet.

4

OF WITCHES AND WINCHMORE HILL

Let us remain at Camlet Moat a little longer. The site is held to be of mystical and religious significance to modern-day occultists, and the trees around the remains of the well have ribbons, rags and pieces of paper tied to their branches as offerings to the spirits they believe dwell there. Pentagrams may also be found, drawn in chalk on some of the trees and although some may regard this as minor vandalism, it is actually a sign that the moat is being watched over and looked after by a group of people dedicated to its preservation. Indeed, when English Heritage wanted to make the site safer for visitors by filling in some of the holes that still remained after Sassoon's excavations of sixty years earlier, they contacted these groups and worked with them to improve the area without upsetting any religious sensibilities.

The writer and ghost-hunter Elliott O'Donnell mentions Camlet Moat in *Ghosts of London* and goes on to relate the story of Geoffrey de Mandeville's treasure and the well, as already examined here in the previous chapter. He later says that the ghost of 'the Witch of Edmonton' is sometimes seen 'prowling the site of the old moat'. He does not specify that the 'old moat' is Camlet Moat, but that would seem to have been his meaning. According to O'Donnell, her ghost is seen near the moat and 'the adjoining roads' as a shadowy figure, bent double and hobbling along slowly and painfully with the aid of a stick. However, there are a couple of problems with this. Either the identity of the shadowy figure has been mistaken, or the location of the moat has been misidentified. There used to be many moated sites around the borough, only a few of which still exist, and O'Donnell's comment that the ghost is seen in the 'adjoining roads' suggests another location surrounded by a network of roads, rather than the remote Camlet Moat which is adjacent to Hadley Road alone, at least a mile from any other road.

In 1970 the *Palmers Green & Southgate Gazette* published an article entitled 'Local Ghosts Walk Again', in which it was stated that the 'Witch of Edmonton' had been repeatedly seen as an apparition surrounded by flames on Southgate Green. However, both of these stories have their roots in folklore and legend rather than fact, although they are based on a very real person.

The Witch of Edmonton is a play written by William Rowley, John Ford and Thomas Decker in 1621 that was based on the real-life trial of a forty-nine-year-old woman named Elizabeth Sawyer from Winchmore Hill, who had been hanged at Tyburn earlier that year. Winchmore Hill was within the parish of Edmonton at the time, hence the title of the play.

Elizabeth Sawyer was born in 1572 and lived in a region of Winchmore Hill woods known then as Lord's Close. She was unfortunate enough to live in a time when the threat of witches and their craft was perceived to be very real. James VI of Scotland had written his *Demonologie*, a very influential book on the subject in the 1590s. When he became King of England in 1603, he brought to the English legal system a greater emphasis on the discovery and persecution of witches. Some of the most notorious English witch trials occurred during James' reign, when any sudden death or misfortune was more likely to be attributed to an act of witchcraft than a disease, infection or simple case of bad luck, and the finger of suspicion would often be pointed at an unpopular member of the local community, or someone with whom the accuser had had a quarrel. Unfortunately for 'Mother Sawyer', she had a very bad-tempered and quarrelsome reputation, which made her highly unpopular, and her physical appearance, described at her trial as 'most pale and ghostlike, without any blood at all, her body crooked and deformed, even bending together', further aroused suspicion.

She had often been accused of witchcraft but there had never been enough evidence to condemn her until a seemingly harmless argument with her neighbour Agnes Ratcliffe sparked off a series of events that would lead her to the gallows.

Ratcliffe was washing clothes in front of her cottage when Mother Sawyer's pig ate some of the soap she was using. She struck the pig with a stick just as Sawyer was coming out of her cottage and Sawyer shouted out to her that that strike would be a 'very dear blow' upon her. Four days later Agnes Ratcliffe was dead; on her deathbed she had accused Mother Sawyer of causing her death by witchcraft. This was evidence enough to bring Elizabeth Sawyer to trial.

Many witnesses gave evidence against her at the trial, but she maintained her innocence throughout and the jury, receiving no guidance from the judge who was sceptical of the existence of witchcraft, was unable to establish her guilt. However, she was taken back to her cell at Newgate gaol, where she was visited by the Reverend Henry Goodcole to whom she made a full confession, detailing occasions when the Devil had visited her and how she had caused harm to others through the use of the powers he had given her. This change of attitude in Sawyer strongly suggests that Goodcole had her tortured and that her confession was thus obtained. Under such circumstances, the poor woman would have confessed to almost any accusation put to her just to end her ordeal. However, unconcerned with how the confession was obtained, it was accepted by the court and Elizabeth Sawyer was hanged at Tyburn, near to where Marble Arch now stands in central London.

Elizabeth Sawyer was hanged at Tyburn in 1621. (© Jay Hollis, 2013)

There were other women from Enfield who were convicted of witchcraft in the early seventeenth century, although execution did not necessarily follow. Agnes Godfrey was accused in 1609 of causing the deaths of an infant and various animals by the use of witchcraft. She was convicted the following year, but seems to have avoided any punishment, for she was accused again in 1621 but acquitted of all charges. Less fortunate was the widow Agnes Berry, who was hanged in 1616 after confessing to using witchcraft to cause a neighbour to become lame and waste away. Again, it is highly likely that her confession was extracted under torture.

It was perhaps unfortunate for Elizabeth Sawyer that the fear of witchcraft may have been more acute in Winchmore Hill than elsewhere in the area due to an event that had happened thirty years earlier in the woods to the north of the village. In September 1590 a group of men were witnessed practising black magic rituals in a place called Hewes Close, near to where Hounsden Road is now situated. A party from Southgate was sent with

bloodhounds to arrest them but the men, having been pre-warned, scattered ratsbane to put the dogs off the scent and fled, leaving an incredible scene behind them. Their pursuers found a cabin that had been built underneath a large tree and on the floor of the cabin various occult symbols and inscriptions had been drawn. They also found a red cockerel and a large crystal on which the word 'SATHAN' had been inscribed. Only one of the culprits was seized, and he was found to have a serpent painted on his chest.

This would be a remarkable and disturbing incident today, but at the end of the sixteenth century it must have terrified the villagers of Winchmore Hill and the collective memory of such an incident would remain for a long time. In the case of Elizabeth Sawyer, who would have been eighteen in 1590, it may have been the case that her neighbours suspected her of being (or perhaps even knew her to be) related to one of the men practising witchcraft in Hewes Close. This is of course mere speculation, but whatever the circumstances, it is evident that she was unfairly treated by her neighbours and no one could blame her ghost for haunting Winchmore Hill.

Perhaps it was no more than a distant memory of 'Mother Sawyer' that gave rise to the belief that the ghost of an old hag haunted a footpath connecting Vicarsmoor Lane with Dog Kennel Lane, now called Green Dragon Lane. According to Henrietta Cresswell (1854–1931) in *Winchmore Hill: Memories of a Lost Village*, this footpath originally crossed an area of common land, appropriately known as the Hagfield, that was enclosed in 1800.

The path, however, remained as a public right of way and was avoided by many after dark because of its reputation. The Hagfield path no longer exists although the right of way continues as a road called Moor Link.

Henrietta Cresswell was famous for her reminiscences of Winchmore Hill, and she mentioned a number of places that had a reputation for being haunted such as the Clapfield Gates, a site that was said to be haunted by the ghost of a black bull. The Clapfield Gates were situated at the entrance to a footpath off Wilson Street, to the north of Winchmore Hill Green. Another reputedly haunted location that she wrote about was the White Lodge, also known as Hope House, a large two-storey house that stood behind a high brick wall on the southern side of Winchmore Hill Road, halfway between Southgate and Winchmore Hill.

The White Lodge was formerly the home of John Heath, who died there in 1838 aged eighty-five, and in the years after his death it was said that his ghost would often be seen at night crossing the courtyard behind the house. A strange apparition was also seen by the White Lodge, by a woman walking home from Southgate after dark. She described what she had seen to Henrietta Cresswell, who recalled the incident many years later in her memoirs. The apparition was dressed all in white, wearing a wide-brimmed hat and a long garment that buttoned all the way from the neck to the hem. Could this apparition have also been the phantom John Heath? In life he had been a dental surgeon with a practice in Hatton Garden, and before that, a naval surgeon under the command of

Houndsden Gutter, near Houndsden Road in Winchmore Hill. (© Jay Hollis, 2013)

Lord Howe. Could the long garment described by the percipient be an old-fashioned coat or smock worn by members of his profession?

On the eastern side of Southgate High Street stands Southgate House. It was built in 1780 by Samuel Pole, who had owned the land since the mid-eighteenth century; it was a family home from then until 1923, when Minchenden Grammar School moved in. The school closed in 1987 and the house is now annexed to Southgate College.

As with most mansion houses of the Georgian and Victorian period, the family of the house lived on the first and ground floors while the servants' quarters were on the second floor, and the kitchens and other work-rooms were in the basement. There have been a number of sightings here of a dark figure who is seen walking along the flagstoned basement corridor. When he reaches the end of the corridor, he simply continues walking - straight through the wall.

The house was owned by a number of very wealthy men before it became a school. Among those former residents was Charles Pole, who died there in 1795, and Isaac Walker, who also died in the house in 1853. J.N. Mappin, one of the founders of the firm Mappin & Webb, was also once a resident. Could it be the shade of one of these men that has been seen? Or, as the ghostly figure has been seen in the basement, perhaps it is the ghost of a former butler or other servant, still carrying out his duties?

St Monica's parish church hall, formerly the Intimate Theatre, on the border between Winchmore Hill and Palmer's Green, is another building said to be haunted. It was built in 1931 and a number of famous actors have performed there, including Vivien Leigh and Roger Moore. In the course of my research I received a letter from a member of an amateur dramatic society that regularly used the hall, stating that an actor suffered a fatal heart attack in one of the dressing rooms during the 1930s and that the room was said to be haunted thereafter. According to my correspondent, the dressing room always feels very cold and the apparition of a middle-aged man in shirt-sleeves has been seen sitting in front of the mirror, putting on his theatrical make-up. Nobody likes to be left alone in that room. The auditorium is also said to be haunted by a ghostly presence.

Finally, an amusing ghost story from 1927. The *London Daily Chronicle* ran an article about Green Dragon Lane, 'a lonely road near Winchmore Hill' being haunted by a 'black form with gleaming eyes' that on a number of occasions had torn the hats off the heads of men walking home alone after dark. Eventually a policeman was stationed near to a gnarled old oak tree, close to where these incidents had occurred. However, Police Constable Gogy had an uneventful evening watching the road, as each passing wayfarer made his way home without incident. Deciding it was all nonsense, he started to make his way back to the police station. All of a sudden, his helmet was knocked from his head and it disappeared into the darkness just as an unearthly scream pierced the still night air.

The terrified constable hurried back to the police station and, an hour or so later, he returned to the old oak tree with the station sergeant and another constable. They waited for the phantom to strike but, again, nothing happened and the sergeant, deciding that he was having his leg pulled, started to leave. Suddenly a rush of air blew against his face and his helmet flew into the road. A terrifying scream sent all three officers into a panic but their fear turned to relief when, a moment later, the moon came out to reveal the ghostly form of a tawny owl flying away from them.

The following morning a search was made of the undergrowth around the old oak tree and the tattered remains of two dozen men's hats were discovered – all the victims of an obsessive owl rather than a mischievous phantom.

5

THE GREEN STREET POLTERGEIST

'Poltergeist' is a German word meaning 'noisy spirit' that is commonly applied to any haunting that manifests in the movement of objects. Such disturbances may be mild and infrequent, while others may be violent and often accompanied by loud, inexplicable noises that terrify the occupants of the building in which the phenomenon is occurring.

Since the late 1970s any book on the subject of poltergeists has usually included the events that took place in a council house in Green Street, Brimsdown, on the eastern side of the Borough. This is because the 'Enfield Poltergeist' is one of the most well-documented cases of its kind, attracting much attention from the national press at the time of the occurrences. Indeed, one of the two main investigators, Guy Lyon Playfair, subsequently wrote a bestselling book entitled *This House is Haunted*, in which he gives a detailed account of the investigation into the events that lasted for over eighteen months.

One night in August 1977, Mrs Peggy Hodgson was a little concerned when two of her four children complained that their beds were shaking. She was at a loss to explain why this should happen and put it down to a childish prank, but what happened the following evening was no prank. She and her children all heard inexplicable noises and loud knockings on the walls. This in itself was very frightening for them, but when a large and heavy chest of drawers moved 18in across the lounge, seemingly of its own accord, they could take no more and fled the house in terror.

They went to a neighbour's house and the police were called in to investigate the 'intruder'. Two police officers arrived and entered the house where one of them, a WPC, was shocked to see a chair move a distance of about 4ft towards the kitchen.

Two days later the Hodgsons, who had moved back into the house, had an assortment of small objects thrown at them by an invisible hand and, in desperation, the police were called again. This time the duty sergeant and another officer arrived and entered the house with Mrs Hodgson who, with the children, was again staying with a neighbour. Mrs Hodgson, reluctant to go far into the house, remained in the hallway while the sergeant looked around the living room and the other officer went upstairs. The sergeant was talking to her when an almighty thudding sound came from the rooms above and he rushed upstairs to see what his colleague was doing. However, the other policeman was not the one making the noise, and neither he nor the sergeant could find the source.

They went downstairs and were discussing the matter with Mrs Hodgson when some of the children's Lego bricks and marbles began to jump up and down. When the toys began flying towards them there was a race to get out of the house first!

A reporter and photographer from the *Daily Mirror*, who had been contacted by a neighbour, also turned up that day and they entered the house, accompanied by the two policemen – only to run back out when the toys started moving again. The photographer tried to take some pictures while he was in the house, but found that his camera was malfunctioning – despite being brand new. Once outside the house, the camera worked perfectly.

The reporter suggested that the Society for Psychical Research should be contacted and they sent Maurice Grosse to investigate. The society is used to receiving reports of haunted council houses and many of them prove to be hoaxes invented by people who simply wish to be re-housed. However, this was not the case at Enfield. Mrs Hodgson told Maurice Grosse that she had no intention of leaving the house, and she stayed there until her death many years later.

Grosse knew he had a genuine case the moment he entered the house and he began what was to become one of the most thorough investigations ever made of poltergeist phenomena. Both he and fellow investigator Guy Lyon Playfair were impressed by the sheer number of events that took place. They estimated that in the first three months of their investigation there had been 1,500 events that defied rational explanation.

These occurrences seemed to be centred on Mrs Hodgson's eldest daughter, Janet, and it was through her that the poltergeist began to communicate verbally with the investigators. At first, strange whistles and barking sounds seemed to be coming either from or just behind her. Maurice Grosse watched Janet closely during these episodes and confirmed that she had no control over the sounds and was not causing them. Over the next few days the noises gradually changed until a rough, masculine voice emerged. It seemed as though the poltergeist had had to learn how to speak – which is, apparently, a common phenomenon with poltergeists.

The voice was that of a bad-tempered and foul-mouthed old man claiming to be the ghost of a former resident who had died in an armchair in the living room. Indeed, a number of the Hodgson family had already seen the apparition of an old man sitting in an armchair and older neighbours confirmed that a previous resident had indeed passed away in such a circumstance. However, the voice would sometimes claim to be someone else. Could there have been more than one spirit 'coming through'? One medium who visited the house commented that every resident of the nearby graveyard seemed to be there!

A close friend of mine used to be a health visitor (she is now retired) and attended the house regularly to check on the children's welfare. She recently told me that on one visit she was chatting with Mrs Hodgson in the living room when she saw a vase moving along the mantelpiece.

'Because I did not believe in any of the tales I put the vase moving along to the vibration of traffic outside, although nothing else on the mantelpiece moved.'

She also remembered that, as she stood to leave, an armchair that had been side on to the window when she entered was now facing her. My friend had not left the room during her visit and neither she nor Mrs Hodgson had sat in the chair, nor had anyone else entered and moved it. She was sure at the time that she had not imagined it or been mistaken.

The events at Green Street lasted for about eighteen months. During this period, almost every type of activity that has ever been attributed to poltergeists occurred in this one case. Objects of all shapes and sizes were moved or thrown by unseen hands; some appeared to hover or fly through the air. Janet herself was seen to float and was also hauled out of her bed and dragged down the stairs by an invisible force a number of times – the deceased old man later said he had done this because Janet was sleeping in his bed.

Apparitions were often seen in the house: there was the old man seen both in the living room and in Janet's bedroom, and there was an old woman, seen by two people, who was angry that strangers were living in her house. However, the most startling apparition was a 'doppelganger' of Maurice Grosse, who was seen by a visitor to the house

looking out of a downstairs window. The visitor was angry that Mr Grosse had not answered the door when she rang the doorbell, but when she asked why he had not done this, Mrs Hodgson explained that he had been upstairs with Janet and herself the whole time. Other occurrences included strange sounds and smells, the sudden materialisation of objects that did not belong to any of the Hodgson family, written messages, the appearance of pools of water and, most alarmingly, the outbreak of spontaneous fires. The house itself – and some of the neighbouring houses – were showered with stones.

However, as the haunting began to 'wind down' and the instances of poltergeist activity gradually became less frequent, it became apparent to the investigators that some of the incidents were being faked by the other children. This often happens as the rest of the children in the house grow envious of the attention being paid to the 'focus' (in this case, Janet). The presence of the media cannot have helped the situation either, as the children would have felt compelled to make sure something happened in front of the cameras (when they were working!). Also, given the reputation of some sections of the British press, it is possible that the children may have been encouraged to fake some of the activities by news-hungry journalists looking for a new twist to the story.

If this is the case, then the newspapers certainly milked their new twist for all it was worth. The Enfield Poltergeist was gleefully denounced in the national tabloid press as a hoax on the basis that some of the occurrences had been faked by the children, even though they had previously reported on events that would be impossible for an adult to fake, let alone a child – how do you shower a house with stones or cause heavy pieces of furniture to hover by themselves? Furthermore, these events had not only been witnessed by the reporters themselves, but also by the police and an assortment of professional people, most of whom, if not all, maintain to this day that what they experienced was genuine.

Over thirty years later, the case continues to fascinate, baffle and divide opinion. The 1992 BBC fictional drama *Ghostwatch* was based on the Enfield case, as were elements of the 1998 film *Urban Ghost Story*, set in a Glasgow tower block. At the time of writing, a British independent feature film entitled *The Enfield Poltergeist* is in production. In 2007 Channel 4 aired a documentary on the case in which a number of witnesses, including Janet Hodgson herself, recounted their testimonies. She agreed to be interviewed after years of requesting that the family be left alone, hopeful that once and for all she could set the record straight and draw a line under it.

6

HAUNTED EDMONTON

If you were to stand in front of the small parade of shops on the north-eastern side of the busy Great Cambridge Road and North Circular Road intersection and look south across the junction, you would see nothing but the constant movement of modern traffic busily negotiating its way around a large round-about surrounded by the conurbation of twentieth-century housing develop-ments. Now imagine you could travel back in time to the year 1900 and stand on exactly the same spot … both of the busy thoroughfares have disappeared and you find yourself surrounded by fields, standing on or near to a country lane, Hedge Lane. A quarter of a mile to the east you will see Millfield House, with the Strand Union and Edmonton Union Workhouses looming in the distance beyond – we will come back to Millfield House later. Even farther in the distance is the Great Eastern Railway line with Upper Edmonton beyond.

However, the first thing you would notice, no more than a few hundred feet to the south, would be Weir Hall, an imposing Victorian mansion house built in the style of a French château. It stands surrounded by its own moat but this is no indication of a more ancient site, for the moat was constructed at the same time as the house, in the mid-nineteenth century. The house looks like it should be haunted, but it is not this house we have come to visit in our search for the supernatural; rather, it is its predeces-sor that we are interested in, and to find that we need to travel back in time again another 100 years…

It is now 1800 and Weir Hall has vanished. All that can be seen to the immediate south is Pymme's Brook cut-ting through the fields, but turn to face the north and you will see an old three-storey Jacobean mansion not far away. This is Wyer Hall. We have at last found our haunted house.

Wyer Hall was built in 1611 by wealthy London haberdasher George Huxley on the site of a medieval mansion he had bought from the Leake family two years earlier. Parts of the previous house, such as the porch and a number of fireplaces, were left standing and incorporated into Huxley's new building. The fireplaces had rose and pomegranate motifs carved into them, the personal symbols of Henry VIII and his first wife Katherine of Aragon, which suggests that the earlier house was built during the first half of Henry's reign. Wyer Hall remained in the Huxley family for four generations before being sold. It then passed through a number of owners and by the early nineteenth century was in a state of dilapidation. It was demolished in 1818.

The story behind the haunting of this house is that there was once a cook employed there who murdered one of the other servants; the room in which the murder was committed was haunted by the ghost of the victim. This particular haunting appears to have been so bad that the room was eventually locked up, and remained so until the house was demolished. This story was recorded by John Philipps Emslie, artist, illustrator and lithographer who, as a member of the Folklore Society, interviewed many people around London and Middlesex from 1860 until 1893 and recorded the folklore that was told to him in his notebooks. He was in fact told two versions of this story; the first, as related above, has it that the cook murdered another servant, whereas the second version, told to him by another person, stated that it was the cook that was murdered by the butler. Either way, it is clear that the murder happened many years before any of the people interviewed by Emslie were born. It seems strange that the room in which the murder occurred should have remained closed despite passing through various owners, unless the room was actually bricked up and forgotten – or perhaps this story was nothing more than a nineteenth-century urban myth (or should that be rural myth?). Emslie made no claim to the veracity of the tales related to him; he simply recorded them as a reference for the future use of other folklorists.

Wyer Hall, 1815. (© Enfield Local Studies & Archive)

Emslie recorded other strange stories about Wyer Hall. In 1872 he was told of a man who was walking home from work one night, carrying a bundle over his shoulder. As he neared 'Wire Hall' (Emslie's spelling), the weight on his back started to get heavier until, walking past the hall, he could barely stand under the weight. Terrified, he cried out, 'Lord 'a' mercy, what's this?' and the weight was lifted as soon as he uttered these words. Emslie was also told of a barn that was all that remained of the old hall complex; this was apparently haunted by the ghost of an Irish labourer who had been killed by a bullock.

Another man interviewed by Emslie in the same year told him how, many years earlier, he had been walking home from The Bull public house one autumn night, accompanied by an elderly man. They were nearing Wyer Hall when the bells of All Saints' church chimed midnight across the fields to the north. Suddenly the younger man saw a large spectral white dog in the road ahead of them. He mentioned this to his companion, but the old man said he could not see it. The man told Emslie that he knew of a number of people who had seen the ghostly dog, and that no harm had ever come to them. He was therefore not afraid, knowing that the dog would simply walk past on its own way. The phantom white dog is one of Edmonton's more well-known ghosts and has been mentioned, albeit briefly, in a number of books and on various websites dedicated to the supernatural. Nevertheless, it would seem that nobody has any ideas or theories as to why a phantom white dog should haunt the area.

Elizabeth Sawyer, 'the Witch of Edmonton' (see chapter four), confessed in 1621 that she was sometimes visited by the Devil in the form of a dog, sometimes black and sometimes white. There is no doubt that her confession was extracted under torture and under such conditions she would have confessed to any accusation put to her. However, her 'confession' would nevertheless have been believed at the time by many people in the area, and the phantom white dog may be nothing more than a distant memory of the events and rumours surrounding her trial. This is perhaps a plausible theory, but it doesn't explain the actual sighting related to John Phillipps Emslie in 1872.

It would be interesting to know if there have been any encounters with the phantom white dog in the years since Edmonton became the densely populated area it is today. When I was at secondary school in the 1980s, I was told by a class-mate who lived in Edmonton that the white dog was supposed to have been seen in and around All Saints' churchyard in Lower Edmonton. I have also been told that the same churchyard is the setting for what must surely rank as one of the borough's most bizarre apparitions – a phantom pair of disembodied legs!

All Saints' churchyard is where the essayist Charles Lamb and his sister Mary are buried, and on the opposite side of Church Street is Bay Cottage, also now known as Lamb's Cottage, where they both spent their final years. They moved from Chase Side in Enfield to Edmonton in 1833, but Charles Lamb was destined to spend little more than a year at the cottage before he died in December 1834. He fell over whilst out walking in Edmonton and grazed his face. The injury was a minor one but he nevertheless contracted an infection in the wound and died two days after Christmas Day, aged fifty-nine.

Mary remained at the cottage until her death thirteen years later. In 1893 the Society for Psychical Research recorded briefly in their journal the case of a Mrs Thomson who lived in the cottage at that time. One evening eight years earlier she had seen the apparition of a man in old-fashioned clothes standing in the passage, and later recognised the figure from a portrait of Charles Lamb that was in a book her husband had bought the same day.

We now move forward 100 years from the entry in John Phillips Emslie's notebook concerning Wyer Hall, to the spring of 1973. Mrs Irene Hickford was trying to sleep in her council house in Chalfont Road, but something was scratching and clawing at her feet and legs under the bedclothes. Convinced there was a mouse in her bed, she removed all the bedclothes and shook them vigorously, but didn't find anything. The following night Mrs Hickford felt the same sensation and tried to convince herself that it was just her dressing gown slipping off the bed and falling to the floor, but the movement continued and she realised it had nothing to do with her dressing gown. Night after night this strange and disturbing phenomenon continued, for months, during which time Mrs Hickford found sleep almost impossible.

Desperate for help, she eventually contacted *Psychic News*, the weekly British spiritualist newspaper that was in circulation from 1932 until 2010, and they put her in touch with the Church of England exorcist Canon John Pearce-Higgins of Southwark Cathedral. He soon ascertained that Mrs Hickford's case was genuine, and he arranged a meeting with faith healers Joan and Ray Broster at their house in August 1974. They performed a simple form of exorcism and that night Mrs Hickford enjoyed a good night's sleep – but the following night the ghost was back and up to its old tricks.

However, on Sunday, 15 September 1974 Canon Pearce-Higgins set up a makeshift altar in Mrs Hickford's sitting room and performed a full exorcism with Mrs Hickford, her son and daughter and the Brosters in attendance. The ceremony was also filmed by a Japanese television crew, who were making a documentary about exorcisms. It lasted about twenty minutes, during which time it was discovered that the ghost was of a woman who had died in the house some years earlier but was trapped and could not find a way to move on. Speaking through the lips of Mrs Hickford, who remembered nothing of the ceremony afterwards, the ghost said that she was trying to get free and had been tugging on Mrs Hickford's leg in an attempt to draw attention to her plight. However, when Mrs Broster asked the ghost to leave, it initially refused and had to be asked three times before it finally went.

The events surrounding the Chalfont Road exorcism were reported the following week in the *Enfield Weekly Herald*. Canon Pearce-Higgins told the newspaper that the exorcism had been a difficult one but that it was 'all in a day's work' for him. He had performed three exorcisms in the previous week alone.

Much of the land around Upper Edmonton was taken up by market gardening until after the Second World War, and there used to be a nursery at the northern end of Dyson's Road, opposite St Mary with St John's church. By the entrance to the nursery stood Pteris House, a Victorian building that was demolished in the 1950s, when the last of the nurseries in the area were relocated to places further away from the centre of London. For many years until its demolition, Pteris House had a local reputation for being haunted. It was believed that the ghost of an old man haunted the house, and strange lights were seen at night around the nursery site. There may well have been a rational explanation behind the cause of these lights, but everyone who lived in the neighbourhood was wary of the house and the area was avoided after dark. One family that lived there used to take in lodgers, but none of them ever stayed for more than a few days and they would all leave in a distressed state.

Another building that has long since been demolished is the Edmonton Empire, which used to stand in New Road, Lower Edmonton. It was built in 1908 and the leading music hall stars of the day regularly filled its bill, none more often than the much-loved Marie Lloyd, who gave her last performance there on 4 October 1922. She had been singing 'It's A Bit Of A Ruin That Cromwell Knocked About A Bit', staggering around the stage as part of the performance – or so the audience thought. She was in fact desperately ill and collapsed as she staggered off the stage into the wings. The audience loved it and cheered all the more loudly, not realising that it was not an act and she would be dead within three days It was not long before rumours began to circulate at the Edmonton Empire that Marie's ghost haunted her former dressing room, and it was seldom used as a result. The Edmonton Empire was turned into a cinema in 1933 and later renamed the Granada. It closed in 1968 and was demolished two years later.

The shade of a little girl in a pinafore is said to wander the rooms and corridors of Millfield House in Silver Street. Her identity is unknown, but it is reasonable to assume that she is an orphan from the mid-nineteenth century.

The date of Millfield House's construction is uncertain. It is first mentioned in 1796 when it was leased to the Russian ambassador by John Wigston, who also owned Trent Park (see chapter two). In 1849 the house was taken over by the Strand Board of Guardians, who opened a workhouse school there. However, the school regime was a particularly harsh and cruel one. Only three years later, an investigation found that the children had been physically and sexually abused and food meant for the children was being stolen by the staff. Millfield House's little ghost must surely be an echo of this inglorious moment in its history.

By 1866, the West London Union workhouse, later known as the Strand Union, had turned the house into a training college and infirmary. During the First World War, Belgian refugees were accommodated at the house until 1917, when the Metropolitan Asylums Board took it over as St David's Hospital for the treatment of epilepsy. The hospital closed in 1971 and Enfield Council turned Millfield House into an arts centre; a theatre was later built within the grounds.

Long before the Millfield Theatre was built, amateur dramatic groups used to rehearse and perform plays in Millfield House – and in fact they continue to do so. A member of one of these groups, Mrs Celia Gooch, sent me a letter in September 2000, in which she told me how she felt that one room in particular, the Bridport Room, had a very depressing atmosphere and no

Millfield House. (© Emma Hollis, 2013)

rehearsals ever went well there. She stated that 'if there was ever any upsets or hysterics, they always took place in this room'. It is interesting to note that she did not know about the little girl and had never experienced anything of a ghostly nature in the house herself. Nevertheless, she was convinced that the house was haunted.

On the opposite side of Silver Street to Millfield House and Theatre is Aylward's School. The Huxley building, previously known as Silver Street School, is the oldest part of the Aylward school complex and is said to be haunted by the ghost of a girl who fell to her death on the stairs. Her final screams and the sound of a girl crying have been heard near the site of the old staircase.

In the next chapter we will visit a haunted house on the north-western boundary of Lower Edmonton.

7

FOOTSTEPS AT SALISBURY HOUSE

Salisbury House, in Bury Street West, is a Grade II★ listed, semi-timber-framed building that is one of the oldest buildings in the borough. The exact date of its construction is not known, but it is thought to have been built either at the end of the Elizabethan period or early in the reign of James I, sometime between 1590 and 1610; it is the sole survivor of the former hamlet of Bury Street.

For most of its 400-year history the house was a private residence, although it was used as a school from 1883 to 1895. In 1936 it was bought by the former Edmonton Urban District Council with the intention of turning it into a museum. However, the house was in such a bad state of disrepair that in 1947 it was considered for demolition. Thankfully this did not happen and ten years later, after some restoration work, it was opened as an arts centre. Enfield Council undertook a further year-long restoration of the house in 1992 and, as with Millfield House, it continues to be used as an arts centre and venue for various societies to hold their meetings.

The house has three storeys, which seems a rather odd proportion for such a relatively compact building, and it is believed that the present structure may have once formed a wing of a much larger building called Bury Lodge that stood adjacent to Salisbury House until it was demolished in 1936. It is not known for certain why the house bears the name of Salisbury, but it is believed that the building was once owned by the Cecil family, successive members of whom have held the title Marquess of Salisbury since the reign of Elizabeth I. Another possibility is that the house may have been part of the nearby Sayesbury Estate and that over time the name has been changed from Sayesbury to Salisbury.

There are two legends associated with Salisbury House. The first is that the notorious Judge Jeffries (1644-1689) lived there for a time. However, there is no documentary evidence to support this theory, although it is known that his daughter lived with her husband at Durant's Arbour in Ponders End (see chapter one) and is buried in

Salisbury House, c.1910. (© Enfield Local Studies & Archive)

St Andrew's church in Enfield Town. This is the only connection the notorious 'Hanging Judge' has with Enfield. The other legend is that there is a secret underground tunnel that links Salisbury House to All Saints' church in Edmonton, over half a mile away to the south. Whilst not impossible, it seems extremely unlikely that such a tunnel would have been constructed over so long a distance, especially considering that Salmon's Brook lays in between the two buildings. Not surprisingly, no evidence of a tunnel has ever been found.

Folklorist John Philipps Emslie (see previous chapter) interviewed a seventy-one-year old man in 1872 who told him about the tunnel and that there used to be 'a great many Roman Catholic Houses, moated about, in the neighbourhood' in

Edmonton. Salisbury House and Bury Lodge, on the outskirts of Edmonton, were once surrounded by a moat that was filled in during the nineteenth century, and there is evidence to suggest that Salisbury House was originally owned by a Catholic family, as there is a priest hole secreted in the basement which was discovered when the 1957 renovation work was being carried out. Roman Catholics were persecuted during the reigns of Elizabeth I and her successor James I, and many families were forced to hold masses in their own homes in secret, conducted by outlawed priests who travelled the country in disguise. It was an act of treason to give shelter to these priests, but that did not deter many Catholic families from doing so, and elaborate hiding places were constructed within

Salisbury House. (© Emma Hollis, 2012)

the framework of their buildings to enable a priest to avoid detection when government officers came to inspect, as they would often do. The successful nature of these hiding places can be determined by the fact that many 'searches' could take up to two weeks without any priest or the religious paraphernalia associated with the Catholic mass ever being found. The downside of this for the priest is that he ran the risk of death by either starvation or suffocation, as sometimes happened. The priest hole at Salisbury House is small and must have been cramped and claustrophobic for any priests that needed to hide in it, but at least it was ventilated by means of a false chimney.

The *Enfield Independent* ran an article about the ghosts of Salisbury House in January 1996, in which a number of people who had previously worked in the house related strange occurrences they had experienced there. Dave Howlett recounted a strange experience that happened one morning as he waited in the house for a student to collect some equipment that had been left there the previous night. He was in one of the downstairs rooms when he heard the sound of footsteps climbing the wooden staircase, and assumed that the student had arrived to retrieve his equipment from the office on the first floor. He heard the footsteps progress along the corridor and enter the office, and this was followed by the sounds of rummaging and furniture being moved around. The student had no business to be doing this and Dave went upstairs to intervene, but when he got to the office he found that it was locked. He then realised that the student would not be able to enter the building without being let in. Dave was the only person in the building.

Footsteps were heard climbing the stairs on another occasion by Jenny Sherlock, who used to serve refreshments at the house. She was talking to a friend on the top floor, where refreshments were to be served while an evening class was being held in one of the rooms on the first floor, when they both heard the sound of footsteps climbing the stairs up to the first-floor landing. The footsteps seemed to stop on the first floor, and sensing that there was something odd about this, the two women went downstairs to see who it was, only to find that there was nobody there. It was later confirmed that nobody attending the evening class had either left the class early or arrived late.

Jenny Sherlock also told the *Enfield Independent* of another incident that took place one Sunday afternoon during a surprise party that was being held for one of the teachers. Both taps on the upstairs sink flew off, sending water spraying in all directions until the flow to the sink could be cut off. However, all was not lost, as there was another sink in the basement and Jenny went down there to use that one instead. When she tried to turn on the water, exactly the same thing happened. Both sets of taps had to be replaced and Jenny joked at the time that

maybe the ghost did not approve of them holding a party on a Sunday.

It seems likely that this incident should be attributed to faulty plumbing rather than a supernatural entity, but what of the footsteps that have been heard climbing the stairs? The staircase is made of wood, a material that expands and contracts with changes in temperature and atmospheric pressure causing audible knocks and cracks, but I do not believe this can adequately explain the sounds that were heard by Dave Howlett and Jenny Sherlock. It seems highly unlikely that any sounds caused by expanding or contracting wood could be mistaken for the sound of footsteps climbing the staircase, especially by two people who would have been used to hearing people walking up and down the same stairway at various times of the day.

Another person interviewed was former caretaker Jean Beadle. She said she was always convinced that there were two ghosts in the house, one male and one female, and she described the basement as having an 'unsettling' atmosphere. She was also accustomed to hearing the rustling sound of a crinoline dress as an unseen woman moved around the rooms on the first floor. Unfortunately, this is the only clue as to who the ghosts of Salisbury House are, as very little is known about its previous occupants, especially of those who lived there in the earlier years of its 400-year history.

8

INVESTIGATION AT THE KING & TINKER

The ancient hamlet of 'Whightwebes' was located at the end of Whitewebbs Lane and consisted of a handful of cottages, a chapel, a large manor house and a tavern called The Bull. All that remains of those old buildings is a cottage and the tavern which is now called the King & Tinker, a name it has carried for many years. The manor house was then known as White Webbs House, which was built in the sixteenth century and given by Queen Elizabeth to her physician, Dr Robert Huike. In 1605 it was used by the Gunpowder Plot conspirators as a safe house, and it was from there that Guy Fawkes made his last fateful journey into London. The house was pulled down in 1790 and a new one, the present Whitewebbs House, was built a quarter of a mile away.

The King & Tinker is the oldest pub building in Enfield and, it is claimed, one of the oldest in England. It was built in the sixteenth century, with later additions, and has a curious entrance porch believed to be taken from the old White Webbs House. The name comes from a ballad that tells of how King James I lost himself whilst out hunting and came upon a tavern, where he fell into conversation with a tinker (a mender of pots and pans). The tinker did not recognise his new drinking companion and said he had never seen a king, whereupon James offered to take him to see the king. They rode off into the woods on James' horse and soon caught up with the rest of the hunting party. James' courtiers dismounted and bowed, and the tinker, seeing so many refined men, asked James which one was the king. James mused that it must be either the tinker or himself as they were the only ones not bowing, whereupon the tinker fell to the ground begging for forgiveness. The king was much amused and rewarded the tinker with a knighthood and yearly pension. It is said that this incident happened at the King & Tinker pub, although another pub near Windsor also lays claim to the legend. However, it is doubtful that the story is true.

In 2012 I was invited to attend a paranormal investigation being conducted at the King & Tinker by North London Paranormal Investigations (NLPI), a group

The King & Tinker in the nineteenth century. (© Enfield Local Studies & Archive)

founded by ex-policeman Michael (aka Mickey) Gocool and his partner Louise. I had not previously heard of the King & Tinker being haunted, so I jumped at the chance to take part in an investigation. Little did I realise at the time that it would be the first of many for me.

I met Mickey, Louise and trainee investigator Lynna in the pub's car park shortly after half past nine on a Sunday evening in April and we chatted for a while outside. Mickey, who is a psychic, told me how he had first become aware of paranormal activity at the King & Tinker in the 1980s when he was sixteen. He had been doing a gardening job in Whitewebbs Park and went to the pub with his colleagues at the end of the day. He thought he was going there to enjoy a drink, but as they arrived he saw something in the car park that greatly disturbed him. Two men were fighting, or rather one man was beating the other senseless and being encouraged to greater levels of violence by a crowd of

men that Mickey described as looking like gentry from a bygone age. At first Mickey thought that what he was witnessing was actually happening. The scene was so vivid that it made him feel sick and scared, but then he realised that nobody else present could see what he was seeing. That scared him even more. This was Mickey's dramatic and rather unwelcome introduction to his psychic abilities.

We entered the pub shortly after ten o'clock and Mickey chose the dining area as the base of operations. Louise set up the monitoring equipment there while Mickey set up a remotely operated night vision camera in the main bar. He introduced me to Barry Duke and his partner Toni, who took over the pub in December 2011. Toni told us that a former chef, who had worked at the pub until only recently, often saw the ghost of a little girl running through the kitchen, always heading away from the main building towards the cellar door. She appears to be about seven years

The King & Tinker. (© Emma Hollis, 2013)

of age and is often seen in the kitchen and sometimes in the toilet block at the other end of the building, wearing a white dress. According to Mickey, who had sensed the little girl on a previous visit, she had been run over by a cart. The accident did not kill her but she was crippled and, unable to earn her keep, was more or less abandoned by her family. She was afraid of Mickey and he could not ascertain how she had died, but it may be reasonable to assume that she died as a result of illness or disease, exacerbated by her condition.

Before the investigation, I accompanied Mickey as he took baseline readings around the building with a thermometer and EMF (Electromagnetic Field) Detector. This is done to establish normal temperature levels and identify sources of electricity that might otherwise be mistaken for evidence of paranormal activity.

It also enabled Mickey to identify the paranormal hotspots where we would be most likely to get interesting results.

We then went upstairs to the living quarters where there are two bedrooms, a bathroom, kitchen, office and living room. Mickey felt nauseous for the whole time we were upstairs and he said that it always happened to him whenever he was in contact with a spirit. We were accompanied by Toni who told us that, with the exception of the living room, she didn't like the feeling in any of the upstairs rooms. It may be worth noting that the living room is in a more recent part of the building, dating back to the nineteenth century, and is separated from the other rooms by a small flight of steps. The room she disliked the most was the office, which has one small window overlooking the entrance porch. Toni

A night-vision image taken during the investigation. (© NLPI, 2012)

told us she has seen 'a large black shadow' rushing past her in this room and, as we stood there talking, Mickey picked up the spirit of a very tall man that he described as being very active. He had the impression of this figure stooping to look out of the small window as if anxiously waiting or looking for someone. Shortly afterwards, as we walked into the second bedroom, Mickey felt a sharp pain in his chest. I noted these incidents down but it was not until half an hour later that we learned of their significance.

We were discussing our findings downstairs with Louise and Lynna when one of the customers, who had stayed behind to help with the investigation, interrupted us. He had overheard our conversation and confirmed to us that Mickey's description of the tall man sounded exactly like a former landlord who had died of a heart attack in the rooms above the pub. This was intriguing as none of us, including the new landlords, had been aware of it.

By now the pub was closed and there were twelve people remaining to take part in the investigation, including the NLPI team and myself. Mickey set up two more remote cameras, one in the kitchen and the other upstairs, and then the lights were turned off shortly after half past eleven.

To begin the investigation a soft toy was placed on a table in the main bar, the oldest part of the building, to hopefully encourage the little girl to interact with us. It was felt that she might be more likely to come forward if another girl spoke to her and Barry and Toni's daughter volunteered to sit at the table and attempt to make contact, while the rest of us remained in the restaurant area. She was monitored via the remotely controlled infra-red camera and was also filmed with a hand-held camera, using a night-vision setting. Nothing much happened during this session apart from some light anomalies, commonly referred to as 'orbs'. These are believed by some to indicate the presence of a spirit but are more often proven to be caused by either the movement of dust particles or insects, or light reflections being picked up by a digital camera (orbs seem to be a phenomenon peculiar to digital technology). Most of the orbs we saw fell quite obviously into one or other of these categories, but others were less easy to explain; there were no draughts passing through the room and yet some orbs were seen to change direction, and some questions appeared to produce a greater number of orbs, as if in response. Coincidence perhaps, but Louise and I noticed something else after the investigation had moved on to the kitchen. The remote infra-red camera was left running and a number of people either stood or sat alone in the main bar at various points during the night. It became apparent that there was a lot of orb activity whenever a female was in the main bar, but almost none whenever there was a man there, and they would disappear altogether whenever Barry went into the main bar.

We watched him go in three or four times and he stayed there for at least five minutes each time. These were the only times when no orb activity was recorded, and we wondered whether it was because the little girl was afraid of men. It was not conclusive proof by any means, but it did seem strange nevertheless.

A similar session was held in the kitchen but with more interesting results; whispering voices were heard by two people and the thermometer recorded sudden drops in temperature, which subsequent investigation could not explain. The hand-held EMF detector also indicated a small column of intense energy that seemed to rise to a height of 3ft or 4ft from the floor – the same size as a little girl perhaps? It proved difficult to gather any visual evidence in the kitchen because both the night-vision cameras failed. The battery in the hand-held camera drained in a very short time despite being fully charged, and the remotely operated camera, which is mains powered, worked for less than a minute. The two-way radio being used in the kitchen also died, despite having a fully charged battery that should have lasted eight hours. This is a common phenomenon in the presence of spirit activity and it is believed that a spirit uses up electrical energy as it tries to materialise or make contact.

Perhaps the most interesting incident of the night happened in the cellar. Louise and Lynna went down there with a digital thermometer and, having noted some temperature fluctuations that appeared to be in response to her questions, Louise tried an experiment with remarkable results. The thermometer's digital display showed the temperature to be 8.5°C and Louise asked the spirit if it could take the

This door is thought to have come from the old White Webbs House. (© NLPI, 2012)

temperature down to 7.5°C. The thermometer's reading dropped slowly to 7.5°C and then stopped. She asked again if the spirit could take the temperature down, this time to 6.5°C, and again the temperature dropped very slowly to the specified level. She then asked for the temperature to be taken down to 4.5°C and then, when the temperature duly dropped by two degrees, she asked the spirit to make it colder still by another two degrees. The cellar was now very cold at 2.5°C and Louise was keen to leave, so she said out loud that if the spirit wanted them to leave, it should make the temperature reading go down to 1.5°C. Almost immediately, the temperature reading shot down to 1.5°C, and the two women quickly thanked the spirit and returned to the restaurant area. This is a remarkable piece of evidence that suggests an intelligence at work.

The investigation ended in the main bar with a Ouija board session involving five participants with the rest of the group, including myself, observing. The session was filmed by Mickey using a hand-held night-vision camera (the lights were still off), and Lynna kept a written record. Contact with a spirit was soon established and, from the responses that were indicated via the board, the name of the former landlord was confirmed. The next question picked up from where Louise's experiment in the cellar had left off…

Do you want us to leave you alone? – YES
Are we making you unhappy? – YES
Do you want us to help you? – NO
Are you happy? – YES
Did you die here? – No answer
Did you live here? – YES
Is there a little girl too? – YES

The questions asked after this point received either no answer or answers that didn't make much sense. The question, 'do you want us to leave you alone?' was repeated and the answer 'YES' was again indicated. Mickey closed the session, and at three o'clock the investigation was brought to an end. A few weeks later I became a member of NLPI and have been investigating haunted locations with them ever since.

9

BEERS, WINES & SPIRITS

The King & Tinker is just one of a number of pubs in Enfield said to be haunted. Another pub, the Rose & Crown in Clay Hill, is reputed to be haunted by the ghost of the infamous highwayman Dick Turpin, and the galloping hooves of his horse may still be heard on the road outside. Fanciful stuff perhaps, but there is a genuine connection between Turpin and the Rose & Crown. It was owned by a man named Mott (or Nott), who is believed to have been his grandfather. If this is true, Turpin would most certainly have made use of the pub when he was holding up coaches in the area. He was captured in York and hanged there in 1739, but his ghost must be a very restless spirit, for there are many other places said to be haunted by him, including The Spaniard's Inn at Hampstead, Aspley Guise Manor in Bedfordshire and various sites in and around Epping Forest in Essex.

Personally, I'm not convinced that Turpin's ghost haunts the Rose & Crown. The details of his appearances there seem to be identical to those at the Spaniard's Inn and it may well be that the story has transferred from one pub to the other over time. However, the Rose & Crown's haunted reputation does not rely on his ghost. Over the years, the staff and the pub's regular customers have maintained that the ghost of a 'friendly female' in nineteenth-century dress has been seen wandering through the oak-beamed rooms, and the ghost of a cavalier is also said to haunt the rooms upstairs. In January 2004 the landlady, Veronica Oakley, told the *Enfield Gazette* that although she had never seen anything she had definitely felt a presence and that she felt the 'friendly female' ghost looks after her and the pub.

The Rose & Crown stands in an area that may have had a reputation for being haunted for many years. The wooded area and road behind the pub is called Beggar's Hollow, once known as Bull Beggar's Hole, which is thought to be a corruption of Bull Boggart's Hole. A bull boggart is an old English term for a phantom or goblin. Perhaps it is one of the Rose & Crown's otherworldly residents that has given the area its name.

The Rose and Crown, Clay Hill. (© Emma Hollis, 2012)

The Crown & Horseshoes is a Grade II listed building on the banks of the New River, near Chase Green on the outskirts of Enfield Town. It has had a couple of black marks in its history: in 1816 the body of the pub's landlord John Draper was discovered down a well in Potter's Bar. His predecessor, James Tuck, was charged with the murder but acquitted at his trial. Sixteen years later, merchant sailor Benjamin Danby was 'befriended' at the Crown & Horseshoes by the men who would later that night slit his throat and rob him, leaving his lifeless body in a road-side gutter. We will look at that particular murder in more detail in chapter thirteen.

However, it is not, as one might expect, either of these murdered men who have appeared in ghostly form at the Crown & Horseshoes. An article in the Christmas 1975 edition of the *Enfield Gazette* told how a regular customer, Brian Bullock, had been waiting for the pub to open when he saw an elderly woman walk past the window. The pub was supposed to be empty and when

the landlord arrived a short while later, he and Brian searched the premises from top to bottom, but no one was found. This seems to have been the only time the ghost was sighted, but she has often made herself heard. The article recounts how, late at night, the cellar door would be heard to slam shut, often many times a night, and the landlords' dog and cat would resolutely refuse to pass this door and descend into the cellar. This was most noticeable in the dog, which would follow the landlord's wife everywhere except for the cellar – it would never go into the cellar.

Apart from a brief period in the 1990s when it was renamed The Enfield Stores, there has been a pub called The Hop Poles on the corner of Baker Street and Lancaster Road since at least 1838, although the original weather-boarded cottage was far older than this date and was a private residence before becoming a pub. The present building was opened in 1909.

In the *A-Z of Enfield Pubs*, Gary Boudier interviewed the then landlord, who knew

The old Hop Poles pub, c. 1890. (© Enfield Local Studies & Archive)

nothing about a ghost when he took over The Hop Poles, but it was not long before strange things started to happen in the cellar. Every night he would personally ensure that the taps were turned off and would turn them back on the following morning. However, on one morning he found that they had already been turned on, and this happened a number of times. He told himself he must have forgotten to turn them off the night before, although he knew he hadn't. The landlord and his wife were soon convinced that their new pub had a resident ghost and they took to referring to him as 'George' so as not to frighten their young children. It is thought that 'George' is the ghost of a former potboy who had been run over and killed a short distance from the pub. He had apparently jumped off a bus when he realised he was on the wrong one (the old buses were open at the back), and was hit by a passing motorist as he ran back across the road. It wasn't until after they had started calling the ghost 'George' that the landlord discovered the potboy's name had been George.

Most of the paranormal activity at The Hop Poles falls into the poltergeist category. In the late 1990s a news crew, who had been permitted to spend the night in the cellar, fled in terror after some beer barrels started to roll around corners towards them. On another occasion, another crew were filming an interview with the landlord when a technician pointed out that the monitor they were watching wasn't actually plugged in. A metal ice scoop has been seen to fly on many occasions across the cellar, glasses have been thrown 6-8ft behind the bar, stirrers have jumped out of their glasses and plugs are habitually pulled out of their sockets – all by unseen hands. Similar activity has occurred upstairs too. According to a local newspaper article from the mid-1990s a succession of barmaids who had rooms above the pub soon chose to live elsewhere because of the disturbances. The Hop Poles' ghost continues to draw interest. Most recently, on Halloween 2012, a media production company hosted a ticketed ghost-hunting event in search of 'George'.

The present pub was built in 1909. (© Emma Hollis, 2013)

By coincidence, the next pub is called The George. Located in the centre of Enfield Town, The George occupies land where an inn has stood since the reign of Henry VIII. Before the Reformation, it was owned by the monks of St Leonard in Shoreditch, who brewed their beer here using locally grown ingredients. During the eighteenth and nineteenth centuries The George was Enfield Town's main coaching inn, but the present building was erected after this period, in the 1900s. In recent years it

The old George coaching inn. (Image supplied by The Enfield Society)

has had a major refit, to the point that its interior is now unrecognisable from the former layout.

It is from The George's coaching days that its ghost story comes. Just ten miles from the centre of London, coaches would stop here for a change of horses and coachmen before either returning to the city or continuing north. On one fateful evening, the coach from London was very late. One of the coachmen waiting at the inn was especially worried, as his favourite horse was part of the team pulling the missing coach. His concern turned to relief when he heard the familiar clatter of horses' hooves and the rumble of the coach's wheels on the road outside. He ran outside to greet the coach, but slipped over on the cobblestones and was trampled to death under the horses' hooves. It is said that a shadowy figure is sometimes seen to run out from the pub and into the road where it vanishes. Interestingly, this bears a similarity to The Hop Poles' story, even to the point that a former landlord used to refer to the ghost as 'Old George'.

10

FORTY HALL'S UNSEEN SERVANT

Forty Hall is a Grade I listed house that was built in 1629 for Sir Nicholas Rainton, Alderman and later Lord Mayor of London. Rainton died in 1646 and the house was inherited by his great nephew, also called Nicholas Rainton. It then passed through marriage, first to the Wolstenholme family and then to Eliab Breton who died in 1785 owing a lot of money (as did his successor, Edmund Armstrong, who died in 1797). The hall was bought two years later by wealthy merchant James Meyer, whose family owned the estate until 1895 when it was bought by Henry Carrington Bowles as a residence for his eldest son, Henry Ferryman Bowles. In 1943 the house passed to his

Forty Hall. (© Jay Hollis, 2012)

grandson, Derek Parker-Bowles, who sold the house and estate to Enfield Urban District Council in 1951. The house has been open to the public as a museum ever since.

The house is surrounded by 153 acres of parkland, all of which is open to the public, and contains clusters of woodland. The largest of these surrounds a man-made lake adjacent to Maiden Brook, and much of the ground to the east of this lake is marked by irregular dips and troughs. This is the site of Elsyng Palace, perhaps the least-known of Henry VIII's palaces.

It is believed that Elsyng was originally a moated house built in the fourteenth century. It was bought in the late fifteenth century by the Chancellor of the Exchequer, Sir Thomas Lovell, who extended and modernised the house. The estate passed to the crown after Lovell's death and, although Henry VIII seldom visited, his children spent much of their young lives there. It was at Elsyng that Prince Edward and Princess Elizabeth were told of their father's death in 1547. The palace continued to be used throughout the sixteenth century and into the seventeenth but, by the time Forty Hall was built, it was in a state of dilapidation and was finally demolished by the younger Nicholas Rainton in 1656 to make way for an avenue of lime trees. The avenue exists to this day, leading up the hill towards the house, although many of the original trees had to be replaced after they were blown down in the hurricane of 1987.

I have long been aware of Forty Hall's haunted reputation. I grew up a stone's throw away and some of my earliest memories are of both the house and the surrounding parkland. According to the ghost story, a young servant girl employed at the hall was severely reprimanded for a misdemeanour. She was upset and ran off to hide in the cellars which, at the time, were being filled with firewood to be stored until required during the winter, some months later. Once full, the cellars were locked up and the unfortunate girl's screams, stifled by the volume of firewood around her, went unheard. It was assumed by the other servants that she had run away, and nobody realised she was in the cellars until they were opened some months later, whereupon her lifeless body was discovered. She had either suffocated or starved to death and it is said that the girl's lonely spirit has wandered the cellars ever since looking for a way out.

It's an intriguing story, but whether there is any truth behind it is debatable. There are no historical records that support it and it seems to me that if such an incident ever did happen, it is more likely to have occurred in the cellars of a much larger building. My suspicions seem to have been confirmed by Vicky Sanderson, Forty Hall's Business Development & Community Access Manager, who stated:

> The story about the maid in the cellar is highly unlikely, given that a house of this size would have been used constantly by servants and the structure of the building, with the cellar rooms being partitioned (only) by the floorboards of the room above, would mean her calls would have been heard throughout the building.

So how did this story come to be associated with the hall? It may well be that it originated in another house, and given the hall's proximity to the site of the much larger Elsyng Palace, it would be easy to see how the half-remembered story of an incident that occurred in the old palace might have become associated with Forty Hall. Then again, the story may simply have been nothing more than a spooky tale to frighten and thrill the children of former residents in equal measure. Forty Hall's manager, Gavin Williams, believes the story may have been invented by a member of the park's authority sometime in the 1950s or '60s.

However, this does not mean that Forty Hall is devoid of ghostly activity. The house has been open to the public since the 1950s and over the years the staff have often been asked if the house is haunted, especially by visitors who have just been on the first-floor landing, where it seems there is a presence that is often felt but seldom seen. Vicky Sanderson told me that the area of the first-floor landing nearest to the stained glass window is most often associated with ghostly activity and that a volunteer once swore there was something or

someone standing next to her when she was locking the window shutters one weekend, even though she was alone.

In 1986 an electrician was on the first-floor landing investigating an electrical fault, and had the uncanny feeling that he was being watched the whole time he was there by what he perceived to be a 'friendly presence'. On another occasion, in 1995, a cleaner was working there when, in the corner of her eye, she saw an arm dressed in a dark shirt complete with buttons. It was as if somebody was behind and to the side of her, but when she looked straight at the arm there was nothing there. She put it down to her own imagination and did not think much more of it at the time, but when the same thing happened to her a couple of weeks later, she became convinced she was seeing a ghost. The same cleaner also found that the bedding on a four-poster bed, exhibited in a first-floor room,

The first-floor landing, before the 2012 renovation. (© Christine Matthews. Licensed under the Creative Commons Attribution-Share Alike 2.0 Generic Licence. To view a copy, visit http://creativecommons.org/licenses/by-sa/2.0/ or write to Creative Commons, 171 Second Street, Suite 300, San Francisco, California, 94105, USA)

The renovated landing reinstates the house's original layout. (© Jay Hollis, 2012)

needed to be straightened out every few days, even though there was a barrier across the open doorway to the room preventing visitors from entering. Every few days she would find the bedding creased and crumpled in the same spot, as if somebody had been sitting on the bed. She could not guarantee that it wasn't caused by visitors going where they shouldn't or another member of staff playing tricks on her, although all the staff swore to her that they hadn't touched the bed, but it seemed odd nonetheless. The same room is now called 'Rainton's Bedroom' and is freely accessible to the public.

On the ground floor there is another room where the sound of excited children screaming, laughing and running around with heavy footsteps used to be heard. It always felt icy cold in the room, regardless of the time of day or the season, but the sounds and the inexplicably low temperature stopped as soon as the room was redecorated and the phenomenon has not been experienced since then.

As with many of the haunted locations around Enfield, it is not known whose ghost haunts Forty Hall, or who the disembodied children may have been. It would seem that nobody has witnessed any apparitions directly, with only the

cleaner seeing the mysterious arm clad in a dark shirt with buttons. The dark attire may suggest a former servant, but there simply is not enough evidence on which to base an identification. Whoever the ghost may be, it is felt by many to be a friendly one, although that did not stop a security guard from fleeing the house in terror one night, when he heard his name being called. He was near the first-floor landing at the time and was alone in the house.

It is not so long since Forty Hall was on the English Heritage Buildings at Risk Register, but due to the dedication and hard work of volunteers and members of Enfield Council, its future is far more secure. The house was reopened in 2012 after the completion of a major renovation project that returned much of the building to how it would have looked in the seventeenth century. The staircase and much of the first-floor landing previously described have been removed, as these were modifications added in 1897, and a reproduction Jacobean oak staircase now stands where the hall's original staircase would have stood, although the section of the first-floor landing most associated with ghostly activity remains intact beneath the stained glass window.

I visited Forty Hall, for the first time after its reopening, in August 2012 accompanied by my wife Emma and our two young children. We looked around the three main rooms on the ground floor and climbed the stairs to the first floor together. Once there, we separated and I wandered the floor with my daughter, making sure we explored every open room, while Emma was dragged through the rooms by our impatient two-year-old son. Consequently, they ascended the staircase to the second floor about five minutes before we did. The route through the house takes you up the main staircase, but the way down is via the servants' staircase, previously closed to the public, which was a relief to Emma. As we climbed the staircase, she appeared with our son on the top-floor landing and said that she was glad we didn't have to go back down the main staircase, as she didn't like the second of the two mezzanine landings before reaching the top floor. When she had stepped onto the landing she felt a sudden rush of adrenaline, as you might experience in a 'fight or flight' situation, and hurried up the remainder of the staircase. This strange occurrence may not be evidence of the paranormal, and I leave it for the reader to make of it what they will; however, it is intriguing that the sensation only happened while Emma was on the mezzanine landing, and she was totally unable to account for it.

In November 2012 I obtained permission for NLPI to conduct an investigation at Forty Hall. The house had never been investigated before and we felt very privileged, but with only four hours available to us, we thought it unlikely that we would get much evidence. The evening was attended by three guest mediums, none of whom had ever visited the house before or knew anything of its history and they all offered a lot of information which was duly recorded. Unfortunately, none of it could be verified. However, there were two moments that stood out for me; one of NLPI's own sensitives, on her first investigation, said that she could 'see' a sorrowful elderly female servant standing by the window on the first-floor landing, looking out. Could this be the spirit that others have sensed?

The other moment was supplied by one of the mediums, Gillian Trench, who felt that 'Rainton's Bedroom' was not the main

Rainton's Bedroom. (© Jay Hollis, 2012)

bedroom of the house, but rather the room where the sick and dying would be looked after. She described a distraught young woman in her early to mid-twenties, suffering from the symptoms of a fever that claimed her life in that room. A few days after the investigation I discovered that all three of Christian Paul Meyer's daughters had died at Forty Hall; Anne Sophia died in 1838, aged twenty, followed five years later by Louisa Joanna, aged twenty-six, and Eliza Maria, aged twenty-one. If Gillian's assertion that 'Rainton's Bedroom' was where the sick would be looked after is correct, could it have been the spirit of one of these tragic girls that Gillian picked up?

At eleven o'clock we reluctantly packed away our equipment and left with our appetites whetted, eager to return. NLPI regard Forty Hall as an ongoing investigation and I will one day publish a full account of our investigations at the hall. Another house we would like to investigate is Myddelton House, less than half a mile to the north-east of Forty Hall and the subject of the next chapter.

11

ENCHANTING MYDDELTON

Myddelton House is a Grade II listed three-storey house that was, for many years, the home of the Bowles family but is now the headquarters of the Lea Valley Regional Park Authority. It was built in 1818 by Henry Carrington Bowles (1763-1830) on the site of an Elizabethan property called Bowling Green House. Henry's wife, Anne, had inherited Bowling Green House in 1809 but, after her death three years later, Bowles had the old house demolished and a new one constructed of white Suffolk brick. He named it after Sir Hugh Myddelton, the engineer who, 200 years earlier, had designed and constructed the New River to supply London with clean water from springs at Amwell, near Ware in Hertfordshire. A loop of this man-made canal flowed through the garden at Myddelton until 1968, when it was filled in. Henry's son, also called Henry, inherited the house in 1830 and he left it to his nephew, Henry Carrington Bowles Treacher, who inherited the house in 1852 on the condition that he changed his name from Treacher to Bowles, thus

becoming Henry Carrington Bowles Bowles. He and his wife Cornelia had five children and Edward Augustus (affectionately known as 'Gussie') was the youngest son.

E.A. Bowles was born at Myddelton in 1865 and died there in 1954 aged eighty-nine. As a young man he chose a career in the church, and took a degree in theology at Jesus College, Cambridge. He abandoned his vocation in 1887 when both his brother John and sister Medora died of tuberculosis. Stricken with grief, he returned to Myddelton where he devoted the rest of his life to developing the gardens. Over the years he became an authority on many species of plant, especially the crocus, and he introduced and successfully grew many of the rarest and most newly-discovered plants. In its heyday, many people came from all over the country to visit E.A. Bowles' garden and by the time he died in 1954 he had been vice-president of the Royal Horticultural Society for twenty-eight years, despite being entirely self-taught. For many years after his death the gardens

Myddelton House, headquarters of Lea Valley Regional Parks Authority. (© Jay Hollis, 2012)

were neglected, but thanks to a Heritage Lottery fund and the dedication of senior gardener Bryan Hewitt, they are being restored to their former glory.

Bryan has worked at Myddelton House since 1982 and has often been asked by visitors if the house is haunted. He believes it is; he was once walking along the path above the orchard when, through the corner of his eye, he noticed a man bending down to pick up an apple. He saw the man clearly enough to discern that he was wearing a dark suit and a boater, but when he turned to get a better look there was nobody there. Had he seen a ghost or had he simply imagined it? If this had been an isolated incident he might have put it down to imagination, but other people have experienced strange things, especially former joint caretakers Ena Cook and her late husband Mike. A few years ago Bryan wrote an article about the house's ghosts for the 'E.A. Bowles of

Myddelton House Society' newsletter, in which he recorded what Ena Cook had told him. A transcription of the article is reproduced here with Bryan's kind permission. She believed there were four haunted places at Myddelton…

One early morning while I was cleaning the ground floor (this was in the early 1980s when there was no carpet in the board room), I saw the lower half of a man in crisp pinstriped trousers and highly polished black shoes, the upper half indistinct, striding from the exhibition room, past the short corridor to the kitchen, heading towards the boardroom, the floor of which Mike had just polished, leaving the polishing machine and hose against the entrance while it dried (to deter anyone from entering the room). I thought it was Geoff Hall and called out to him not to go in there, but the figure carried on noiselessly into the boardroom. I rushed in there to tick him off – but there was no sign of him!

Another time, this time on the top floor, at the northern end of the house at the front (this used to be Mr John's room, E.A. Bowles' brother, who tragically died of tuberculosis, aged twenty-seven, in 1887), Julie (Ena's daughter) was cleaning the hall outside the big room when she heard muffled noises and laughter coming from it. It was night-time and everyone had gone home. Puzzled, she told me and we both heard the chatter together. I turned the handle, opened the door and the noises stopped! The light was on but the room was empty. Florence Darrington was maid to Mr Bowles from 1925-1945 and lived on the top floor during that time. Shortly before she died in 1999, aged eighty-eight, she told me, 'At the end of the house was Mr John's room. I felt it very uncanny there. Although I hadn't seen anything I found that somehow I felt a presence which made me hurry back to the main part of the house.'

For a time Mike regularly saw, from the large bay-windowed room on the first floor looking down on the stable yard, oil lamps flickering in the early morning light and figures reflected against the walls he believed to be stable lads talking and laughing, and sounds of hooves on cobbles. One day he told Alan Moss (who was at that time Treasurer of the Lee Valley Regional Park Authority) and, doubting him, Alan came in early to see for himself. He was shocked to witness the eerie ritual with Mike. They both came down and advanced on the mysterious lights in the chill winter air dimly illuminating the old stable yard but as soon as they crossed the threshold of the gates the lights were extinguished 'like a candle'.

One evening, one assistant care-taker called Sylvie was in the small corridor near the kitchen when something 'pushed her'. She complained of feeling freezing cold, her eyes were popping and her usually curly hair seemed straightened! She kept repeating, 'something pushed me!'

Eddie Piggott, gardener at Myddelton from 1968-1982, was walking the central path of the pergola, past the Old Enfield Market Cross, when he heard footsteps close behind him. He turned suddenly to see a lady in a crinoline dress for a few moments before she evaporated. He saw her a few times. The same lady was seen by a four-year old girl 'Evie' in the 1990s, who was seen chatting to the invisible lady. Mike had seen her too.

I contacted Bryan Hewitt in December 2011 and he very kindly offered to show me around the house. We met on a par-ticularly wet and windy day, in the week before Christmas, and he introduced me to Terry Oliver, who has been the caretaker since September 2010. I would describe both Bryan and Terry as down-to-earth men, not predisposed to flights of fancy, but they are convinced that Myddelton House is haunted. Terry told me that on his first evening he was being shown his duties and had just been in the large room on the top floor known as 'Mr John's Room', as mentioned in Bryan's article. This room is in a wing of the house that was built by E.A. Bowles' father and the floor level is slightly higher than the older main part of the house. Terry had just descended the two steps that lead into the top-floor corridor when he heard a friendly female voice say 'Hello' to him. He told me that the voice was right by his ear, as if the

The stable block and courtyard, where strange lights have been seen. (© Jay Hollis, 2012)

speaker was standing very close behind him, and he assumed that a member of staff was introducing themselves to him. However, when he turned to see who had greeted him, the corridor was empty. Straight away the hairs on the back of his neck stood on end, although he felt more exhilarated than scared. He had not been told that Myddelton had any ghosts but immediately thought the house must be haunted and has been convinced ever since his first day.

Another incident happened to Terry one evening after seven o'clock as he was locking up the house. He begins this process on the top floor, ensuring that all the lights and appliances are switched off and all the doors locked, systematically working his way down the building. On this particular evening he had descended the stairs to the ground floor, having secured the two floors above, when he heard the sounds of somebody walking around somewhere in the house above him. Assuming that he must have missed a late worker or that someone

had entered the building to retrieve a forgotten laptop, or maybe some documents, he made his way back up the stairs, turning the lights back on and unlocking each room as he made his way back through the house to make sure that nobody had been inadvertently locked in any of the rooms, or was wandering the corridors – but he found no one. Furthermore, anybody wanting to leave the building would have had to have sought Terry to let them out, but nobody did.

Bryan showed me around all the places in the house where strange incidents have happened, including the short corridor on the ground floor where the assistant caretaker Sylvie had been pushed by an invisible force, and where Ena Cook had seen the curious apparition of a man whose upper half was blurred while the legs and feet were clearly visible. This corridor connects the main corridor with the small kitchen and is so short that Ena must have been no more than 6ft away from the figure.

The second-floor corridor where Terry Oliver had his first strange experience. (© Bryan Hewitt 2013. Reproduced with the permission of Lee Valley Regional Park Authority)

Bryan Hewitt recommended that I should interview one of the cleaners, Sarah Scales, who has worked every morning at Myddelton House, from six o'clock until a quarter-to-nine, since 2009. She told him of a number of strange experiences she had had in the house. When I contacted her, she told me that she sometimes feels uncomfortable when working in the second-floor corridor and on the landing by Mr John's Room, as well as inside that room. At such times she has the unnerving impression that she is being watched by a man.

One morning, while cleaning on the first floor, Sarah was startled by the loud scream of a woman coming from somewhere nearby. There were two other women working on the same floor, but both of them swore they had not made such a noise. On another morning she was using the vacuum cleaner in the house when, in the corner of her eye,

she saw something white move quickly past her. She had a quick look around but could not find anything or anyone that might explain the movement.

The old stable block now forms part of the new visitor centre. As mentioned in Bryan's article, strange lights and shadows have been seen here in the stable courtyard, seemingly caused by oil lamps, accompanied by the sound of horses' hooves on the cobbles. However, if somebody goes to investigate, both the lights and the sounds cease as soon as that person passes through the stableyard gate. It is in the stable block that Sarah is sometimes aware of the smell of horses, which might not be so surprising, were it not for the fact that there have not been any horses stabled here since the 1930s. The stable block adjoins the newly-built visitor centre and museum, and Sarah told me of another curious incident that took place here. She had finished cleaning the floor in the cafeteria, which is decorated with large ornamental vases containing dried grasses and flowers, and had gone into the next room for a few moments. On returning a short time later, she found a long green leaf from one of the vases lying in the middle of the floor that had not been there when she left the room. There was no apparent reason why this should have happened; the design of the vase was such that its contents could not possibly have fallen out, nobody else had been in the room, and there was no breeze or wind that could have dislodged the leaf. It looked to Sarah as though it had been deliberately placed on the floor for her to find.

Perhaps the most disturbing incident to have happened to Sarah occurred opposite the visitor centre, in the new Abercrombie Building, which is used for horticultural studies. Sarah was cleaning in one of the rooms one morning when she felt somebody grab her hips from behind. Surprised, she spun around, but was even more shocked to find that she was alone in the room. Crucial to these incidents is the fact that she had no knowledge of Myddelton's history or of any ghostly stories associated with the house until after she had spoken to Bryan Hewitt on the matter.

Have any of Myddelton's ghosts been identified? Bryan concluded his article by saying that he believed there was 'a benign and kindly spirit' watching him and his colleagues in the gardens and, if this is the case, it would seem most likely to be the spirit of E.A. Bowles who continues to keep an approving eye on the gardens he created and loved so much. It is thought that the disembodied voice heard by Terry Oliver on his first day may have belonged to E.A. Bowles' sister Medora, who nursed her brother John through the illness that would claim his life. In doing so she caught tuberculosis from him, and succumbed to the disease herself a few months after her brother in 1887. John was twenty-seven when he died and Medora just nineteen. It is tempting to speculate that these two lives, cut so tragically short, continue to echo through the rooms and corridors of Myddelton House. They were both buried with their parents in St Andrew's churchyard, Enfield Town. It may be interesting to note that Medora's death mask was kept in a locked room next to Mr John's Room for many years until E.A. Bowles ordered that it should be destroyed, shortly before his own death. Could it also be the ghost of Medora that has been seen in the gardens?

The Lea Valley Regional Park Authority website describes Myddelton House Gardens as 'an enchanting place

Myddelton House and Gardens. (© Jay Hollis, 2012)

to visit', and this is no hollow boast. The house is used as offices and is not open to the public (although the ground floor is opened to the public on one day of the year in September as part of the 'Open House Weekend'), but the newly-restored gardens are open every day, except for Christmas and New Year's Day, and are well worth a visit. In the visitor centre and museum you can learn the fascinating story of the life and work of E.A. Bowles, while in the garden you are free to explore the places he created, such as the rock garden, the alpine meadow, the kitchen garden, the stone garden, the carp pond and the Enfield Market Cross, which stood in the market place in Enfield Town from 1826 to 1904 and was saved from demolition by E.A. Bowles.

It would seem that Myddelton is so enchanting that some of its former residents cannot bear to be parted from the place, even after death. So if you do visit and you catch a glimpse of somebody dressed in old-fashioned clothes, taking in the tranquil surroundings, don't be too surprised if that person suddenly vanishes when you look straight at them.

12

THE GHOSTS OF CAPEL MANOR

Whenever Hilda Warren visited her bachelor brothers James and John at Capel House, they would always take great pleasure in teasing her about the phantom old lady that haunted the second floor. Not that Hilda was particularly frightened; she'd never seen anything, after all. Nevertheless, ghosts have been seen at Capel Manor.

Capel Manor house is located immediately north of Bull's Cross, not far from Myddelton House. The earliest record of a manor in this part of Enfield, on the northern border of the modern borough, dates back to the thirteenth century when it was held by an 'Ellis of Honeyland'. The manor was owned by the Capel family for a relatively short time – from 1486 to 1546 – but the name 'Capel' has remained ever since this period. The old manor house was demolished in the mid-eighteenth century and two new houses were constructed, one by Robert Jacomb, who took ownership of Capel in 1745, and the other by a Mr A. Hamilton. Jacomb's house was called Capel House but when Rawson Hart Boddam bought

the manor in the late eighteenth century he chose to have this building demolished and lived in the house built by Hamilton, renaming it 'Capel House'. This is the present building, which is now the headquarters of Capel Manor Horticultural & Environmental College. My enquiries about Capel's ghostly old lady put me in contact with the college's principal, Dr Stephen Dowbiggin, to whom I am very much indebted for the following information. He told me that there are frequent instances of paranormal activity in the house, including numerous examples of doors opening on their own. He believes there are at least three ghosts at Capel Manor.

James and John Warren may have been merely teasing their sister, but there is nevertheless a particular room on the second floor where the ghost of an old lady has sometimes been seen, sitting in a rocking chair – although more often the sound of the chair rocking is heard without any visible manifestation. The ghost is apparently that of a former nanny to the Warren family, tea merchants who

Capel House in 1873. (Image supplied by The Enfield Society)

lived for a time in Assam, India. When they came back to England they brought the nanny back with them to Capel House, where she remained long after her charges had grown into adulthood and eventually died in the house.

Some years ago a party was held in the house to celebrate Stephen Dowbiggin's birthday. One of the guests, Stephen's nephew, was known by some to possess psychic abilities and he was asked light-heartedly if there were any ghosts in the house. Without any prior knowledge of any ghosts at Capel or the history of the house, he proceeded to wander from room to room, sometimes running his hands along the walls or over pieces of furniture. He was accompanied by a group of guests who were naturally intrigued at the outcome but most viewed the exercise as just a bit of fun. Every room was declared to be devoid of any ghostly presence – that is, until they came to the old nanny's room. In this room Stephen's nephew

calmly said that there was an old lady who was very happy in the house and who said she lived there. At this point a woman in the group that had gathered in the room fainted and the impromptu ghost hunt was swiftly brought to a close.

The old nanny is not the only ghost to have been seen at Capel Manor. College staff and students have occasionally seen the shade of a smartly dressed elderly gentleman, sitting in the library. Those who have seen this apparition say that he most closely resembles Colonel Sydney Medcalf, the last private owner of Capel House, who lived there from 1932 until his death in September 1958. According to Stephen Dowbiggin, Colonel Medcalf's ghost was seen recently by one of the office staff in a first-floor corridor. Apparently, he looked as shocked as she did!

In the late 1980s a paranormal research group conducted an investigation at Capel Manor. Thermometers were placed around the house and 'traps' were set up

Capel House, c.1950. (Image supplied by The Enfield Society)

with cameras and tape-recorders – all the usual paraphernalia associated with ghost-hunting. They also held a séance on the top floor in an attempt to make contact with the old lady in the rocking chair. They were unsuccessful in contacting her but did manage to contact another spirit who was very keen to talk to the medium holding the séance. The spirit of this man claimed to be a former gardener who had had an affair with the daughter of the master of the house (or one of the house's predecessors). The lovers planned to elope, but when the master discovered this, he had the gardener murdered and his body dumped in a well. He then told his daughter that her lover had left without saying goodbye in return for money. She remained unmarried and never discovered the truth.

In March 2013 I was told a slightly different version of this story by Peter Everett, who lives nearby in Bull's Cross, in which the spirit that had been contacted was the daughter. She had married her lover before he was murdered and dumped in the well, which was then filled in, and her spirit remains restless until her husband's body is recovered. Peter's reason for telling me this story was that he had seen the 'White Lady of Capel' for himself…

One night forty years ago he was driving home and, as he reached his destination, his headlights caught a woman dressed in a long, white, old-fashioned dress crossing the road that runs beside Capel House. She was walking away from the house and passed straight through the wall on the opposite side of the road. Two years later she was seen again by a couple of people who lived in cottages in Whitewebbs Lane, but the most curious incident happened to Peter's neighbour about five years ago. He was outside his house on a warm night when an agitated woman in modern clothing approached him and begged him to help her husband who she said was trapped down a well. Peter's neighbour was naturally concerned and offered to call the police, but in the brief moment that he looked away from her, the woman had vanished!

Stephen Dowbiggin told me that three old wells have been discovered in the grounds of Capel Manor, only one of which has been excavated; no bones were found in it. It is not known whether there are any bones in either of the other two wells but it may be presumed that the White Lady and the gardener still haunt Capel Manor, as no bodies have yet been discovered.

Capel Manor College offers an extensive range of courses in horticulture, animal care, saddlery, garden design, groundsmanship, arboriculture, countryside management, floristry and even balloon artistry. The house is not open to the public, but Capel Manor Gardens is open every day from March to October. The gardens occupy a 30-acre site with over sixty specially designed gardens and landscapes for visitors to explore, and the college hosts a number of events in the grounds throughout the year.

13

'A MURDER OF THE BLACKEST DYE'

The Enfield Chase enclosure map of 1777 shows a road running west to east across the chase from the Great North Road at Monken Hadley, north of Barnet to Parsonage Lane, near Enfield Town. This route corresponds to the route now formed by Hadley Green Road, Camlet Way, Beech Hill, Hadley Road, Lavender Hill, Holtwhite's Hill and Parsonage Lane. This is the route of the old Barnet to Enfield Road.

In *Ghosts of London*, first published in 1932, the ghost-hunter and author Elliott O'Donnell relates an incident that happened on this road in Enfield to a man named Ward. The sun had just disappeared below the horizon on an autumn evening in the latter half of the nineteenth century (O'Donnell did not specify a date but it can be assumed that the incident took place sometime before Parsonage Lane and Holtwhite's Hill were developed in the late nineteenth century) and Mr Ward was accompanying his uncle, a travelling salesman, in an open carriage. Sections of the road passed through wooded areas and as they passed beneath the darkened trees,

the encroaching silence was broken only by the clatter of the horse's hooves and the rumble of the wheels.

A feeling of intense sadness seemed to settle on the two travellers and then, suddenly, the horse shied and bolted, galloping off at breakneck speed. Mr Ward's uncle was barely able to control the animal and the two men clung on to the carriage for dear life. It was only when they emerged from beneath the tree cover into the moonlight that they could see what was terrifying the horse so much, for there was a man walking calmly and silently alongside the carriage, effortlessly keeping up with them despite their speed. His face was deathly white and he had a deep, bloody, gaping wound across his throat. This ghastly apparition accompanied the two travellers until they had passed a particular gate, by which the phantom stopped, and it was only then that the horse became calm and slowed to a trot. Looking back, Mr Ward and his uncle could see the ghost standing motionless by the gate and then it gradually faded before their eyes.

The following day they were told that the stretch of road where they had experienced their ordeal was the site of the murder of a man named Danby, who had been robbed and killed in 1832. A tree near to the gate where the apparition had stood had an inscription carved into the bark marking the spot where the murder was committed, and the road had a reputation for being haunted by the ghost of the unfortunate victim.

The murder of Benjamin Couch Danby is little remembered today, but it made national headlines in 1832, and a lengthy folk song was composed in which it was described as 'a murder of the blackest dye'. Danby was a twenty-seven-year-old sailor who had returned to England from the East Indies. On his return he found that his father, a legal wig-maker in Temple, had died earlier in the year, leaving a substantial amount of money to his two sisters but only an allowance of one guinea a week to him. The reasons for this are unclear. It may be that his father had been unhappy with his son's choice of career, or perhaps he knew that Benjamin could not be trusted to handle large sums of money responsibly, as the events that preceded his murder would prove. Maybe Benjamin had already made plenty of money at sea and his father did not consider it necessary to leave him a large sum. Whatever the circumstances, Benjamin Danby had plenty of money with him on the evening of 19 December and did not mind who knew it.

He was staying with his cousin Hannah, who had recently married Peter Addington, a baker who lived in Chase Side, not far from the Crown & Horseshoes public house by the New River. On that fateful evening he was in the tap-room of that pub playing

Cottage adjoining the Crown & Horseshoes, c.1900. (© Enfield Local Studies & Archive)

dominoes for pints of beer with Charles Jackson and the pot boy, Joseph Matthews. A twenty-nine-year-old gardener by the name of William Johnson was also invited to play but he declined, saying that he had no money. However, Danby offered to pay for him if he lost and – not for the first or last time that night – he took a silk net purse from his pocket containing a large number of coins. Johnson agreed to play and joined them. They had only been playing for fifteen minutes when Matthews was called away and his place was taken by a man named Richard Wagstaff.

At around nine o'clock Johnson stopped playing and his place at the table was taken by another man, John Taylor. By this time Samuel Fare had entered the bar. He was an unemployed twenty-two-year-old who was receiving money from the parish. An hour later the landlord looked in and found that a number of men, including William Johnson and Sam Fare, were lying asleep across the chairs. He woke them up and admonished them for using his home as a doss house, whereupon Fare became aggressive, producing two shillings and sixpence to prove that he could pay for a drink. While this was going on, at about ten

The Crown & Horseshoes today. (© Emma Hollis, 2012)

minutes past ten o'clock, John Cooper, an eighteen-year-old who worked in the brewery on the opposite side of the river, entered the pub. At some time after half past ten, having finished arguing with Fare, the landlord told his wife not to serve them any more beer and went upstairs to bed. Danby, who by now was very drunk, told them not to worry and bought them all a half pint of gin. His generosity was to be his undoing.

At ten minutes past eleven Danby left the pub accompanied by Richard Wagstaff, William Johnson, John Cooper and Samuel Fare. He could barely stand and the landlady told Joseph Matthews to help him over the bridge across the New River, lest he should fall in and drown. Matthews asked Sam Fare to see the gentleman safely home and Fare took hold of one of Danby's arms while Johnson took the other. The group left the pub together, but Richard Wagstaff left them when they reached his house a 100 yards or so away from the pub. Before going indoors he quietly told Cooper not to go with Fare and Johnson, as he had a feeling that they were going to rob Danby, but Cooper refused to heed his advice and caught up with the three men as they continued along Chase Side. They were pushing and shoving each other boisterously as they went and a brief scuffle broke out, during which Sam Fare fell to the ground. When he got up he bade the others a good night and left them.

The group now consisted of Danby, Johnson and Cooper. When they came to the house where Danby was staying, Johnson asked if he would come with him to Pinnock's beer shop at the top of Holt White's Lane (modern Holtwhite's Hill) to get a pint of beer. 'Yes, with all my heart,' replied Danby. So they carried on walking to the crossroads and turned left to climb the hill.

However, unbeknown to the others, Sam Fare had already stolen Danby's purse and it was not until they were half-way up the hill that Johnson, who had been carefully feeling through Danby's pockets while supposedly helping him to walk, realised this. Johnson suddenly turned around and said to Cooper, 'I will be damned if Sam has not robbed him.'

In a fit of rage, Johnson tripped up Danby and threw him against Cooper, who fell into the ditch by the side of the road with Danby on top of him. Cooper struggled out from under Danby but his cap was still under him and when Cooper retrieved it, it was soaked in blood.

'What have you been doing?' said Cooper to Johnson. 'Don't kill him!'

Johnson was on top of Danby. He got off him and held out a knife to Cooper.

'You take this knife, and go and finish him; I have began him.'

Cooper refused to take the knife and Johnson went back to Danby, who was groaning.

'What will you give?'

'Oh, don't hurt me; Oh, don't...' pleaded Danby.

'What will you give?' repeated Johnson.

'Anything.'

Johnson turned to Cooper and said, 'Don't you say a word – don't tell anybody.' Cooper then heard Danby make a horrible gurgling sound as Johnson slit his throat with the knife. The two men ran back down the hill leaving Benjamin Danby's lifeless body lying face down, half in the road and half in the ditch.

The body was discovered at half-past five the following morning by a labourer on his way to work and William Johnson, John Cooper and Sam Fare were all arrested later the same morning. John Cooper offered to turn King's Evidence against the others when he was arrested, an act that may well have saved

The Enfield Murder, 1832. (© Victorian Picture Library, www.victorianpicturelibrary.com)

his neck. The three men were tried at the Old Bailey in the first week of January the following year; Johnson was found guilty of the murder and sentenced to be hanged, while Cooper and Fare were acquitted, although Samuel Fare was found guilty of robbing Danby and for that was deported to Australia.

The above sequence of events is based on the evidence given by Cooper and accepted by the jury at the Old Bailey. Unsurprisingly, it exonerates him from any involvement in both the robbery and the actual killing but Johnson's final confession, which was made after he had been condemned to the gallows, tells a different story. According to Johnson, he and Danby were walking alone, Cooper, Fare and Wagstaff having gone their separate ways, when Danby told him that he had been robbed. Johnson was frightened that he might be accused of highway robbery if he left Danby alone and wanted to take him to a place of safety, but Danby told him that he did not wish to go back to his cousin's house as he was loath to wake them up. Cooper re-joined them five minutes later but when Danby saw him, he accused Cooper of being one of the men that had robbed him and flew at him in a rage. In the scuffle that followed, all three men fell into the ditch and Johnson claimed that it was Cooper who carried the knife and was the first to cut Danby. Johnson confessed that he then took the knife from Cooper and also cut

Holtwhite's Hill. (© Emma Hollis, 2012)

Danby, although he did not know what had possessed him to participate in the killing. He ended his confession by stating, 'I now leave this world for a crime which I shudder at.'

Whichever version of the events preceding the murder are to be believed, it is clear that Danby died from the final wound inflicted upon him by Johnson – something that Johnson himself did not deny. Less clear is the role that Cooper played. If Johnson told the truth in his confession, then Cooper got away with murder. If other people in the area believed this, is it any wonder that the site of the murder gained a reputation for being haunted by Benjamin Danby's restless spirit?

14

THE OLD FIRE STATION

Benjamin Danby's grisly apparition is not the only ghost to be associated with Holtwhite's Hill. Further down the hill is an old fire station, built in 1936, that was used as the headquarters of the Enfield branch of the Royal British Legion from 1972 to 2012. During this period there were numerous reports of paranormal activity from the staff and club members. The club had its main bar on the ground floor with a large function room and bar upstairs. It is in the upstairs bar that most of the incidents, usually in the form of poltergeist activity, were reported and this area was originally where the firemen's dormitory and living quarters were.

In 1976 the *Enfield Gazette* interviewed the head bar steward, Wilf Jones. He stated that he had, on a number of occasions, heard a glass being smashed in the upstairs bar whilst it was locked and shuttered up. He would investigate immediately, having to unlock the bar to do so, and sure enough, there would be the shattered pieces of glass on the floor, but there was never anyone there.

The only explanation offered for this is vibrations caused by passing traffic, but that is unlikely to have been the cause as the building is of a very sturdy construction and the windows are double-glazed. However, another incident that could not be attributed to vibrations happened just a week or so before the *Enfield Gazette* article was published. Wilf was cleaning in the upstairs bar when the telephone rang, and he stopped what he was doing to answer it. Whilst on the phone he watched in surprise as the bucket of water he had left on the bar, about 9ft away, was slowly lifted into the air by an invisible hand and then crashed to the floor. Wilf stated that he had become used to clearing up after the ghost, who staff had taken to nicknaming 'Fred'.

On another occasion, Wilf entered the spirit cellar and switched on the light to see a man wearing a white shirt and black tie standing in the corner. Surprised, he asked the man 'what the hell' he was doing there but was then even more shocked to see the man disappear. Wilf ran out of the room, terrified, but when he had calmed

Enfield Fire Station, 1936. (© Enfield Local Studies & Archive)

down shortly afterwards, he could find no rational explanation for what he had seen; there was only one way in or out of the spirit cellar and none of the other people working in the bar that day had seen anyone but him come out of the room.

This was one of just a few times that 'Fred' has been seen, but his presence has often been felt and heard by a number of people, mostly in the upstairs areas where unseen heavy footsteps have been heard. In the same article, Wilf Jones' wife Eileen recounted how she was standing on a chair whilst working alone in the upstairs kitchen when she heard the bar door open and footsteps cross the hall. The kitchen door then opened and someone, or something, touched Eileen's back, causing her to spin around and fall off the chair – but there was nobody else in the room.

Another unsettling experience happened one afternoon to a committee member who was checking the decorations that had been set out in the upstairs hall in readiness for that evening's annual 'Navy Night'. The decorations were made up of flags of every nation, and as the committee member wandered around the room, making sure that everything was in its proper place, the flags began to flutter violently as if in a strong breeze – even though there was no breeze in the room. He hurried out of the room and refused to ever go back in there on his own again.

No one knows who 'Fred' was, but there are believed to have been three deaths on the site. In the days when the building was an active fire station, a fireman was crushed below the waist by a fire-tender and another death occurred during a party being held in the upstairs quarters, when a woman stumbled and fell head-first down the hole where the fireman's pole was situated. The third death was of a British Legion bar steward, who died of natural causes in the cellar.

Paranormal research group ISP (In Search of Proof) conducted an

Former Royal British Legion Club. (© Emma Hollis, 2012)

overnight investigation into the British Legion building in 2009. They held vigils in the downstairs bar, the upstairs function room and even the loft space but, despite some anomalous temperature readings and a recorded voice, the results of their investigation were inconclusive (although their report makes for a very interesting read). I have listed the URL for their online report at the end of this book.

When I joined North London Paranormal Investigations (NLPI), I began seeking permission to investigate locations in Enfield. The Royal British Legion building was high on my list, but the need to conduct an investigation became all the more urgent when it was announced that the club was to close and the building sold. In the nick of time NLPI were given permission to investigate the site in October 2012, less than a fortnight before the club's closure.

On the night we were greeted by the club manager, Maria Hamer, who showed us around the most active areas. She told us that the upstairs function room is where the Legion committee used to hold their meetings, but it was eventually abandoned in favour of the downstairs bar, as the glasses behind the

locked upstairs bar would move around and unnerve the staff. At the far end of the function room is a double door, beyond which is small corridor leading to a service lift, the fire escape and the ladies' toilets. Many people have expressed a dislike of this corridor and the two psychics present at the investigation agreed that the area had a very heavy and negative atmosphere. At the bottom of the stairs is a room that was originally the fire station office, and later the British Legion committee room. Maria told us that this room is always cold, defying any attempt to heat it. It was now mainly used for storage and as a changing room for bands performing at the club.

The NLPI investigation proved to be as frustrating as the ISP investigation, although a number of incidents are worthy of note. In the upstairs function room, lead investigator and psychic Michael Gocool picked up the spirit of a former club member who had been taken ill on the premises and died shortly afterwards. Maria had known this person and was able to verify the information given, but our subsequent attempts to establish

NLPI members at the Royal British Legion, Enfield. (© NLPI, 2012)

Many have commented on the oppressive atmosphere in the upstairs corridor. (© NLPI, 2012)

communication via a voice recorder and electro-magnetic field (EMF) meter, with which we had obtained some remarkable results at other locations, were fruitless.

At midnight the investigation moved downstairs and a Ouija board session was opened in the main bar, but this failed to produce any meaningful results. However, a camera was set up in the ladies' toilet after it had been noticed that a toilet roll and cubicle door had been moved during a period when nobody had been in there. The camera itself was then found to have been moved some time later. The ISP team experienced similar activity in the downstairs ladies' toilets three years earlier. Meanwhile, my wife Emma and her sister Victoria, both NLPI members, went back

upstairs, armed with a night-vision camera and EMF meter. They sat in the dark corridor for half an hour with the camera running and nothing much happening. Suddenly there was a loud banging against the fire escape door, and the two women decided to make a hasty exit. This happened after one o'clock in the morning and, although it cannot be guaranteed that there was nobody on the other side of the door, everyone involved in the investigation was accounted for.

At the time of writing it remains to be seen what will become of the building now that the British Legion have vacated it. Whatever happens, I will be intrigued to learn if 'Fred' continues to make his presence felt.

15

THE UNKEMPT MAN

It was late one night in 1958, or at least it was late enough for a six-year-old boy to be in bed and fast asleep and, as far as his parents were aware, that was exactly what Jim Mattingly was doing. However, although he was in bed, Jim was very much awake and reading by the light of a torch. He held the torch close to the page so that there were no chinks of light visible from under the door to give him away. Not that he would be caught, for he could hear if anyone was climbing the stairs or walking past his door, and he would turn off the torch in good time to avoid detection. But everything was quiet and he continued to read.

After a while he stopped and looked up. Had he heard something? No, and yet he felt as though he was being watched. He tried to continue but could no longer concentrate on his book. Slowly, he lifted the torch to illuminate the rest of his bedroom and was horrified to see the ghostly figure of a tall, unkempt and bearded man standing at the foot of his bed. He was scared and quickly buried himself under the bedclothes, with the

torch still on. There he stayed until he eventually fell asleep.

This was the first sighting of a ghost that was to be seen by no less than four members of the Mattingly family in their house in Bush Hill Park at various times over the next fourteen years. The family moved into the house shortly after it had been built in the mid-1950s, and it was not long after Jim had had his first encounter with the ghost that the Mattinglys' eldest daughter Jill also started to see the man, although being three years younger than Jim, she was too young to think it was something to be afraid of. As she grew up in the house, she always maintained that it was haunted, even if her parents did not believe her.

When Jim Mattingly told his parents what he had seen they dismissed it as nothing but childish imagination fuelled, no doubt, by his illicit midnight reading sessions. However, his father Alex was forced to change his mind one night a few years later when he saw the ghostly figure for himself at the foot of his own bed. It appeared so clearly to him that he was convinced there was an intruder in the house, and he searched everywhere but found no one. Furthermore, all of the doors and windows were safely secured and intact.

The fourth member of the family to see the ghost was another of the Mattinglys' three daughters. In the summer of 1971, twelve-year old Susan woke up the rest of the household with her terrified screams, having woken up to find a man standing at the foot of her bed. She was so scared that even her mother, who had thus far remained sceptical, now believed that the house was haunted. The following morning Susan was able to describe the man she had seen; a tall and unkempt bearded man wearing a garment that she described as looking like an anorak without a hood. She also said that, although she could not see the man's legs clearly, she was sure he was wearing something more akin to leggings rather than trousers. Susan saw the ghost again a few days later but this time was not frightened by it.

The story came to the attention of the *Enfield Gazette* the following year and they ran an article about the haunting entitled 'Shadow That Appears in the Night at Bush Hill'. They suggested a handful of clues that might explain who the ghostly figure is.

The Mattinglys' home is one of a number of houses built on the site of a Victorian house called Riverside, which was built in 1874. Another old house, Bush Hill Park mansion, was built in 1685 for East India Company merchant Sir Jeremy Sambrooke, and demolished in 1927. It stood on the other side of the road from where the Mattingleys' home was later built and was at the centre of a vast landscaped estate that contained many outbuildings and a separate banqueting hall that was destroyed by fire in 1837. Could the ghost be that of a labourer employed at one of these houses, or somebody who lost his life in the fire? The descriptions of his clothing seem to suggest a man from an earlier period, probably the sixteenth or early seventeenth centuries, or possibly even earlier. The area is believed to have once been part of the kitchen garden of Enfield Palace, which stood half a mile to the north in Enfield Town, where Pearson's department store is now situated. Mrs Mattingly told the *Enfield Gazette* that she thought the ghost might be a gardener or labourer from this period.

Another explanation may be provided by the proximity of the Mattinglys' house to the New River, a man-made canal designed and built by Sir Hugh Myddleton in 1613 to supply London with clean water from springs at Amwell, near Ware in Hertfordshire. Its construction was a major feat of engineering, using gravity and the natural contours of the land to deliver the water to its destination in Clerkenwell, and it has been suggested that the apparition could be that of a man who lost his life whilst that part of the river was being constructed. However, there are no historical records to confirm any of these theories and the man's identity must remain a mystery.

I had the pleasure of speaking to Alex Mattingly in 2013. He was happy for me to relate this story and confirmed that everyone in his family continued to see the 'unkempt man' long after the newspaper article had been published and that other people have seen him in the area too. Apparently, he still puts in the occasional appearance.

16

THE HAUNTED RIDGEWAY

The Ridgeway is an ancient trackway that once crossed the Enfield Chase. It remained little more than a muddy track until the mid-nineteenth century but is now a major thoroughfare running approximately four miles along a high ridge, as its name suggests, from junction 24 of the M25 London Orbital motorway at the north-western corner of the borough to its end at the top of Windmill Hill, a mile to the west of Enfield Town.

There are a number of reputedly haunted locations along the length of this road and the first of these, travelling south into the borough, is North Lodge, which currently houses St John's senior school. There were four hunting lodges built within the Enfield Chase; South Lodge, East Lodge, West Lodge (now the site of West Lodge Park hotel) and North Lodge. Each of the original hunting lodges was demolished in the eighteenth century to be replaced by larger mansion houses. North Lodge, on the northern side of the Ridgeway, was built by James Brydges, first Duke

of Chandos, who had made his fortune as Paymaster General during the reign of Queen Anne. In 1728 he sought permission from George II to build a new lodge near Old Pond with ten smaller lodges elsewhere around the Chase. His request was denied, but the house near Old Pond was nevertheless built; this became North Lodge.

In 1975 the *Enfield Gazette* published a letter that the editor had received from Mrs Eileen Spicer, who had been born at North Lodge in 1892, the youngest daughter of Sir William and Lady Gundry. She recounted how the grounds were said to be haunted by the ghost of a white horse which, it was believed by the family and staff, was supposed to have been the same horse ridden by Queen Elizabeth I when she hunted at Enfield Chase. As a child, Eileen would often hear the sound of horses' hooves in the evening, galloping up the drive to the house. Thinking that this was her father returning from Enfield, she would run to the front door to greet him, only to find that there was no one there.

The Phantom Horse of North Lodge (artist's impression). (© Jay Hollis, 2013)

Some years later, the Gundry's gardeners were digging in the garden and discovered the skeleton of a horse. Lady Gundry insisted that the bones be given a 'decent burial', and the phantom horse was never heard again. Were these bones the physical remains of the ghostly horse? It seems a possible explanation, although there is another horse buried in the grounds. On the lawn directly in front of the house, under a Spanish Chestnut that is believed to be the oldest tree in Enfield, there is a grave that bears the following inscription: 'ROSIE' DIED 16TH MAY 1894 '11 YEARS A FAITHFUL COMPANION'. Could 'Rosie' be the phantom horse?

St John's Senior School Headmaster, Andrew Tardios, has told me that the sound of horses' hooves has often been heard since the school took over North Lodge in 1993. In that year a security guard became so afraid that he called the police and refused to come into work the following day, and in 1999 a geography teacher was woken by the sounds of horses galloping outside. Mr Tardios also told me that the ghostly occurrences at North Lodge are not just restricted to the grounds:

Inside the building, three different teachers swore that they heard and felt children were running around laughing and giggling and touching the teachers' trouser legs. Knocking on doors late at night is also heard. This is not a boarding school, so it was not a case of pupils late at night playing pranks on the teachers.

The strong smell of pipe smoke has been reported in the headmaster's office when no one has been smoking anywhere near there (and it would now be illegal to do so) and a science teacher, who apparently remains sceptical about the existence of ghosts, once witnessed a fork fly across the kitchen while he was alone in the room.

A mile or so further along the Ridgeway, next to Chase Farm hospital, is an ambulance station. In October 1987, the *Enfield Gazette* reported on the 'strange goings on' that had been happening for many years at the station. Footsteps had been heard frantically pacing around the empty loft space above the depot, mysterious shadows were seen to pass by the office when nobody had actually walked past, the ambulance radios switched themselves on for no apparent reason, and on stormy nights the doorbell was rung repeatedly by an unseen hand. The ambulance garage also had what the *Enfield Gazette* described as an 'authentic cold spot', and one worker related how he would get a 'really eerie feeling' whenever he walked past the cold spot and no longer went past there on his own. A cold spot is a small area that feels significantly colder than the space around it, where no rational explanation can be found to account for it. They are often recorded as evidence of ghostly activity, but should be regarded with some caution as they

are also very difficult to authenticate. According to ASSAP (the Association for the Scientific Study of Anomalous Phenomena) a 'cold spot' usually does not register on a thermometer, and can be caused by a variety of natural phenomena, such as draughts, convection and humidity that may not necessarily be obvious to a person experiencing such a seemingly unexplained drop in temperature.

The ambulance station was built in the 1950s and was originally run by the former Middlesex Council. Back in those days the nightshift workers would take the occasional nap in the ambulances while not required for duty. One man who did this got the shock of his life when a sudden blast of ice-cold air woke him up. He opened his eyes to see the gaunt, wizened face of an old man staring down at him intensely. The nightshift worker fled the ambulance in terror, vowing never to sleep there again, and from then on the other members of staff were reluctant to go into the garage alone. However, despite the eerie feelings and occasional scare, the staff do not feel that the ghostly presence is a malevolent one, but rather an earthbound soul, lost, afraid and unable to progress to the next stage of its spiritual development.

Why should a ghost haunt the ambulance station? Could it be the spirit of a man who died in the back of one of the ambulances as it rushed to the hospital, or could the haunting have a much older origin? The article in the *Enfield Gazette* stated that the station was built on the site of a mass burial ground for victims of the plague and offers this as the only possible explanation, but I am not convinced by this theory. There are various locations around Enfield that are rumoured to be the sites of plague pits, the most persis-

The Ridgeway Ambulance Station. (© Emma Hollis, 2013)

tent being Chase Green, to the West of Enfield Town. However, when I enquired with the Enfield Archives office, they confirmed that nobody knows for sure where any of them were located and that the Chase Green rumour came about as there used to be a pest house on the site that was demolished in 1910.

Thomas Westwood (1814-1888) was a poet and author who lived in Enfield for the first thirty-one years of his life before moving to Belgium in 1845, where he remained until his death. He was a frequent contributor to Oxford University Press' *Notes & Queries* and one of his letters, sent from Brussels and published in 1873, told of a curious incident that happened to him whilst still living in Enfield, although he did not confirm the year. He had been invited to a dinner party by two elderly spinster sisters who lived in a large old weather-beaten house on the edge of the Chase, and walked there late one autumn afternoon as the sun was setting. He described his journey as lead-ing him 'up a steep ascent of oak avenue, opening out at the top on what was called the 'ridge-road' of the Chase' and given that he would have set out from Chase Side where he lived, I believe it is likely that he walked up Holtwhite's Hill.

When he arrived at the house, Westwood was shown to an upstairs room so that he could change his dress for the dinner party. Once alone in the room, he became aware of a faint sound which he described as 'a sort of shuddering sound, as of suppressed dread'. He ignored it at first, thinking that it must be caused by the wind blowing down the chimney or some other perfectly natural phenomenon, but the sound always seemed to be very close to him, no matter which part of the room he stood in. In fact, it was as if the sound was following him. He was unnerved by this and hastily finished getting ready, so that he could leave the room to join his hosts and the other guests in the drawing room below. However, as he left the room and descended the stairs he found that the strange melancholic sound remained with him, and at moments when the conversation flagged during the dinner, he could still hear it, so close to him that it sounded as if somebody was sitting in the same chair, breathing and sighing in his ear with barely contained horror. Looking around the table, it seemed that none of the other guests could hear the sound and it was only him that was being harassed. The evening came to an early end and it was with great relief that he left the house and the distressing sound behind, thankful that he did not have to spend the rest of the night there.

The next time that Thomas Westwood met the two sisters was at a different location and he told them what he had experienced when he had last visited them. They both laughed and told him that they were not surprised as they had often heard the same sound and had grown used to it. The strange sound would sometimes be quiet for weeks, but at other times it would follow them from room to room around the house, as had happened to Mr Westwood. They could offer him no explanation as to what the phenomenon was or why it should happen.

So where exactly did this curious incident occur? Westwood described the house as being old and weather-beaten, and located on or near the 'ridge-road' of the Enfield Chase. It is also most likely that he visited the house at some point before 1845, the year he moved to Brussels to begin a lengthy career, first as secretary and then director of an Anglo-Belgian railway company. Nineteenth-century Ordnance Survey maps of the area show a number of large houses along The Ridgeway, but only a few of these existed before 1845, and less still could be considered 'old' in that year. Another clue contained within Westwood's narrative is the fact that the front of the house was east-facing, but this is as much information as he gives and it is therefore impossible to say with any certainty which house he was referring to.

However, if I was asked to speculate, I think a possible contender may be 'Ridgeway Oaks', a house that stood in its own grounds at the junction between The Ridgeway and Hadley Road for at least 150 years before being demolished in the 1950s. There were a number of grand old houses around the borough that suffered this fate in the early post-war years, and the only surviving clue to the existence of Ridgeway Oaks is a small gatehouse on Hadley Road. The rest of the estate lies under modern housing.

17

GHOST'S AT WORLD'S END

World's End Lane connects Enfield Road to the former Highlands Hospital, now a residential estate, with Winchmore Hill and Southgate beyond. The area around the lane to the north of the old hospital site is known as World's End and sits in a valley formed by Salmon's Brook, with Enfield Town a mile away to the east and Oakwood a similar distance to the west. It is thought that the area came by its name due to its remote location in days gone by, and nineteenth-century Ordnance Survey maps show the lane to be a dead-end track that splits into two footpaths. One of these has since been widened to become Bincote Road, while the other still exists as a public footpath.

This footpath was the scene of a tragic murder that took place in 1909 when Sidney Bunyan slit the throat of his nineteen-year-old sweetheart, Lucy Smith. Bunyan killed his girlfriend as part of a suicide pact, but could not take his own life and so turned himself in to the police instead. He was tried at the Old Bailey and given the death penalty, but was later reprieved and his sentence commuted to life imprisonment. However, facing the prospect of spending the rest of his life behind bars, he killed himself at Maidstone Gaol four years later. Despite the sadness of this tale, it is not the tragic lovers who haunt this area, for the ghost that has been seen not far from the site of the murder would seem to be a monk, suggesting a much older origin.

The only intriguing landmark on the old Ordnance Survey maps is a moated enclosure and this, unlike many of the old moated sites in Enfield, still exists. Other sites – such as Durants Arbour in Ponders End and the Oldbury Manor site to the east of Enfield Town – were filled in and built over in the early twentieth century but the moat at World's End was spared this fate, by being part of the land bought in 1893 by the newly formed Enfield Golf Club. The moat has remained a feature of their golf course ever since.

In the course of my research I was put in touch with Martin Harrow, and I recount some of his experiences here with his kind permission. He was born and grew up in Enfield, and has had a

Salmon's Brook, flowing through Enfield Golf Course. (© Jay Hollis, 2013)

varied career, including a number of years as a news cameraman. His memoirs, entitled *Don't Play with the Harrow Kids*, are an entertaining and frank account of a childhood full of dubious antics, and brushes with the law. It seems that he was often up to no good and frequently somewhere he should not have been. One such place was the private land of the Enfield Golf Club course.

One clear, moonlit evening in the 1960s Martin and a friend were crossing the golf course, unconcerned that they were trespassing on private land. They often did this, and took a perverse pleasure in antagonising the greenskeeper whenever they could. In the distance, on the opposite side of the fairway, they spotted a figure moving up the hill away from the moat, through the out-of-bounds grass. Thinking that it was the greenskeeper, they shouted out in an effort to get him to chase them again and, sure enough, he changed direction and headed towards them. Through the

darkness the figure came closer, and the two boys realised that it was not the greenskeeper, for it was dressed in a large black hooded cloak and seemed to be pushing a mist before it. This was strange enough but what really unnerved them was the fact that the figure appeared to be floating towards them.

His friend turned and fled, but Martin wanted to see into its face. As the figure approached, he did just that and what Martin saw terrified him – in his own words, he saw 'a mass of pulverised flesh being eaten by maggots'. Martin quickly caught up with his friend and they both ran home to his parents' house where Martin's mother, a nurse, treated them both for shock.

Very little is known about the old moat and it is therefore impossible to connect this terrifying apparition to any events in the moat's history. It is believed by some to be the location of a plague pit but, as discussed in the previous chapter, there is no evidence to support this theory.

A phantom monk (artist's impression). (© Jay Hollis, 2005)

The description of the ghost suggests a monk, and there may be some evidence to support this, as the moat – which is fed by Salmon's Brook – is less than half a mile upstream from the site of Old Park Grange – now lost beneath the 1930s housing development of Grange Park. A Grange was a farm that served a monastery and was run by monks, so it is feasible that the terrifying apparition could have been that of a medieval monk.

In *Don't Play with the Harrow Kids*, Martin mentions a number of personal supernatural encounters. As a young child he used to play with other children in the garden of his grandparents' house in Tottenham, but it wasn't until he was older that he realised the children he had played with were ghosts and only he could see them.

As an older boy he was with a group of friends, pushing a bicycle along the road close to Highlands Hospital. They could hear a car approaching them but, as there was a heavy fog, they could not yet see if it was a rich person or the police – nobody else had cars in those days. They were watching for the car when a woman sud-denly appeared from nowhere, ran across the road in front of them and disappeared through a thick hedge bordering the hospital, despite there being no gaps in the hedge. Almost immediately the car appeared through the fog and screeched to a halt alongside the children. It was a police car, but the officer driving was not interested in what the children might be up to, for he got out of the car and very excitedly asked them, 'Did you see that?' before jumping back into the car and speeding away.

Martin told me that the apparition of the woman was often seen by the hospital engineer, a friend of his. The engineer's room would turn very cold, seconds before the woman floated past and through the wall. She was then seen to enter a large oil tank, but never to emerge from it. This ghost's passage through walls and other objects suggest that its origins are from a time before the hospital was built.

Martin also told me that the house in Roundhill Drive where he lived as a child was haunted by the spirit of a council worker who had committed suicide there. The haunting would manifest as a dark shadow-figure descending the stairs. Another place that Martin used to live, a flat in Coverack Close in Southgate, often had the inexplicable smell of oranges, pipe tobacco and burnt toast, and a friend of his once saw a man sitting in the living room who disappeared in an instant. Martin believes this may have been the spirit of his deceased uncle trying to contact him.

It would appear that Martin inherited his psychic abilities from his mother, who was a nurse at Highlands Hospital. She once told him that when a patient had died she would often go to change the bedding on the empty bed, only to find

Highlands Hospital, c.1900. (© Enfield Local Studies & Archive)

Highlands Hospital today. (© Jay Hollis, 2012)

an apparition of the recently deceased patient sitting quietly on, or standing by, the bed. She would calmly explain to them that they had died and that they needed to go 'towards the light'.

Highlands Hospital was originally opened in 1887 as the Northern Convalescent Fever Hospital, for patients with infectious diseases. It was closed in 1993 and converted into residential apartments, but Martin has heard rumours that ghostly activity continues to happen there. I would be very interested to hear from any residents that can confirm this.

18

THE GHOST TRAIN OF HADLEY WOOD

There have been many reports of ghostly activity associated with the railways. There are haunted stations, haunted engines and carriages, apparitions that have been seen on the tracks and even phantom trains. One curious example of the latter forms the basis of a ghost story associated with Hadley Wood, on Enfield's north-eastern border.

One would imagine a phantom train to take the form of an old steam engine, wreathed in billowing clouds of steam, but the train seen on this occasion was a diesel locomotive. Most people would have seen this train and thought nothing of it, and had it not been for the fact that it was observed by two railway enthusiasts, the strange circumstances of its appearance would never have come to light.

Hadley Wood station is on the East Coast Main Line, in a cutting between two tunnels that are simply called Hadley Wood North and Hadley Wood South; each of these comprises of two tunnels. The original tunnels were opened in 1850, but this created a bottleneck when the line was expanded to a double track

(two tracks for the local trains that stop at every station, and two for the main line express between London and the North East), and a second pair of tunnels was constructed and opened in 1959 to accommodate all four tracks.

In September 1980, the two enthusiasts were watching for trains from a bridge that spans the line 600 yards or so to the south of Hadley Wood South tunnel. The sun had only just dipped below the horizon, and they were preparing to leave as they observed one last local train slow to a halt at the signals between the bridge and the entrance to the tunnel. Suddenly they heard a familiar and distinct sound, quite unlike any other train. From behind them came the loud rumble of the twin eighteen-cylinder Napier diesel engines that powered the Deltic locomotives. This was a real treat; the Deltic fleet was at that time being decommissioned, and although some of them were still running, they were all soon be taken out of service. The train passed beneath them with a loud roar and disappeared into Hadley

Hadley Wood South tunnels. (© Emma Hollis, 2013)

Wood South tunnel. The two friends dutifully noted down the name and number in their books – one final treat before making their way home.

Had it not been for their encyclopaedic knowledge, the paranormal significance of this event would have passed unnoticed. However, a doubt was nagging at one of the men and he asked his friend if he had noted the number of the train. '55020' came the reply. They had both seen the same name and number on the side of the engine, and that was the moment when they realised something was not as it should have been, for the Deltic locomotive 55020 *Nimbus* had been broken up for scrap at the end of January that same year, seven months earlier. Indeed, it was the first of the Deltics to be cut up. They went straight to Hadley Wood station, on the other side of the south tunnel, to ask if any unscheduled trains had passed through but none had,

and there had definitely not been any Deltics through in either direction.

Nimbus had a seventeen-year career that began in December 1962 and ended when it was withdrawn from service in December 1979. The Deltics were all named after classic racehorses and were a common sight on the East Coast Main Line during that time, hauling the express trains between London and Edinburgh. They were unpopular with railway enthusiasts when they first came into service, as the fleet of twenty-two Deltics replaced fifty-five much-loved steam engines, but over the years many developed a soft spot for these mighty workhorses and were sad to see them go when they were replaced by the 'Intercity 125' locomotives. It seems that *Nimbus* was also reluctant to go.

Or was it? The Hadley Wood sighting was first reported in issue seventeen of the Deltic Preservation Society's magazine *Deltic Deadline*, published

Nimbus at the Doncaster scrapyard in December 1979. (© 2013. – 53A Models of Hull Collection; the late D.R. Vickers)

in October 1980, and the story was later included in a compilation of true ghost stories entitled *Ghost Trains* by E.H. Herbert. However, it appears that the original story was nothing more than an affectionate work of fiction, commemorating the demise of the first of the once mighty Deltic fleet to be scrapped. So that solves that mystery … although it should perhaps be mentioned that there are people who claim to have seen *Nimbus* elsewhere around the national rail network, in places such as Crewe and also in Derby, where a man once claimed to have seen it passing through the station in 1992. These sightings have led to wild speculation on the internet as to the 'true' fate of 55020 *Nimbus*, including a conspiracy theory

that suggests she was secretly bought by the Ministry of Defence and used to transport military hardware around the country. Despite these rumours, the Deltic Preservation Society maintains that *Nimbus* was broken up in Doncaster in January 1980.

A number of Enfield's older ghost stories, such as the manifestations of Mother Sawyer's ghost (see chapter four) are more legend than fact. The Hadley Wood story, which I do not believe was a deliberate hoax, was mistaken for fact and subsequently found its way into a number of publications on the subject of true ghostly encounters. I have included it here as an intriguing example of a modern legend. It seems you can't keep a good ghost story down.

19

INDUSTRIAL SHADOWS

In the course of my research into the ghosts of Myddelton House I spoke to Sarah Scales, who worked there as a cleaner. She told me that she is sensitive to psychic phenomena, and had experienced a number of strange incidents in the house, all of which I have detailed in chapter eleven. Towards the end of our conversation she told me that the place where she had previously worked was also haunted …

Before being employed at Myddelton House, Sarah had worked evenings at the offices of a factory in Duck Lees Lane, Ponders End – close to the River Lea and the eastern border of the borough. She told me the people who worked there often saw apparitions that would disappear as suddenly as they had appeared. One such apparition was that of a figure wearing a white jacket, but none of the people in the building at that time owned such a garment, and no intruder was ever found. One worker saw a man he did not recognise disappear around a corner at the end of a corridor. There was nowhere for this

person to have gone other than into the ladies' toilets and yet there was nobody in there – the only other option was for the figure to have passed through a solid brick wall. On another occasion a face was seen peering out of one of the office windows, when the building was known to have been empty.

Sarah told me of a rumour among the staff that the factory had been built on the site of a graveyard. However, she was not sure if there was any truth behind it, and I think it unlikely, seeing as the area was a marsh prior to industrial development in the late nineteenth century. Not a particularly good location for a graveyard.

The building may not have been built on the site of a graveyard, but it does occupy the site of the Edison Swan (or Ediswan) United Electric Light Co. complex which, incidentally, is where the three girls that saw the phantom black coach in 1899 worked (see chapter one). All but one of the original factory buildings have long been demolished; the only survivor was built in 1890 and stands not far from where Sarah worked. Could it be

Built in 1890, this building is the sole survivor of the Ediswan factory. (© Emma Hollis, 2012)

that some of the Ediswan factory workers are still wandering the buildings they would have known in life, even after those buildings have been replaced?

In *Dark Journey*, psychic investigator and President of the British Psychic & Occult Society David Farrant writes about another haunted factory building that used to stand by the River Lea in Ponders End. It was built in the 1870s as part of the Corticine Linoleum Company factory, and originally contained a large open space in which long strips of newly-made linoleum could be hung from the ceiling to dry. There was a narrow walkway running around the top of the walls to enable workers to facilitate this. The building was sold in 1936 and modernised to include a first and second

This blue plaque is the only evidence of the site's importance. (© Emma Hollis, 2012)

floor, served by a goods lift, within the space. It was used in later years as a warehouse for the packaging and distribution of machinery components and building materials.

Farrant interviewed a former employee, Eddie Wooll, who had worked at the warehouse for eleven years from 1977, and was told that the building was well known for its ghostly activity, most of which occurred on the top floor. It was always cold there, despite regular attempts by heating engineers to solve the problem, and boxes that had been left neatly stacked on a Friday night would often be found the following Monday lying open with their contents scattered across the floor. The lights on the top floor would switch themselves on and off and a shadowy figure sometimes startled the workers.

The drivers would come in on Saturday mornings to wash their vehicles and, on one occasion, one of them brought his dog with him. He told his colleagues how his dog could always find him, and demonstrated this by hiding in various places in the factory. Sure enough, the dog would run straight to where its master had concealed himself. That was until he hid on the top floor. The dog stood at the base of the staircase and became very agitated, refusing to go up, even when its master appeared at the top of the staircase.

On another occasion Eddie was working late in a first-floor office while another worker, the only other person in the building, was moving stock on the top floor. He could hear a banging noise that told him a metal barrow with a broken wheel was being used, and he wondered why his colleague was not using a different one. Eddie stepped out of the office but was shocked to find his colleague downstairs, where he had been for at least fifteen minutes. They both quickly grabbed their coats and left, without pausing to turn the lights off. Another incident happened during a stocktake when a man fell from a ladder. He landed on top of Eddie and was not hurt, just badly shaken – especially as he had felt somebody push him off the ladder.

In the early 1930s, when the building was still used for the hanging and drying of linoleum, two men fell to their deaths from the high walkway whilst attempting to repair a stuck roller. Could this incident provide an explanation for these events? We may never know, for the building has been demolished and the area is now being redeveloped.

20

SHADOWS ACROSS THE BORDER

Our journey around Enfield's haunted places has come to an end, but there are a number of sites located just over the borough's border that are worthy of note, and I have listed them in clockwise order around the edge of the borough.

Theobalds Park, Cheshunt

Theobalds Park House, built in 1763 with later additions, stands to the immediate north of the Enfield border in Hertfordshire, between the M25 motorway and Cheshunt. The Meux family, who amassed a fortune in the brewing industry, occupied the house from 1820 to 1929. It was then used as a hotel until 1938, when it was sold to Middlesex County Council for £50,000. It was occupied by the army during the Second World War and has been both a secondary school and a residential college since then, but it is now a hotel again.

In 1878 Sir Henry Bruce Meux married Valerie Susie Langdon, a nightclub hostess and former barmaid. A few years later she was running the estate, overseeing extensions to the house and hosting lavish parties. She died in 1910, and it is believed to be her ghost that has been seen descending the main staircase.

Other incidences of ghostly activity have been reported at Theobalds Park. Apparitions have been seen wandering through two adjoining rooms, while in another room guests have had objects fly out of their hands, seemingly of their own accord. In yet another room, said to be the most haunted, guests have had their bedclothes pulled off in the middle of the night by an invisible hand and disembodied male voices have been heard whispering. Some members of staff are reluctant to be alone in this room, and a number of guests have felt so disturbed they have asked to be moved.

Gilwell Park

The ghost of Margaret Chinnery has been seen walking in the grounds of Gilwell Park, near Sewardstone in Essex. She lived there from 1793 to 1812 and transformed the grounds into fashionable gardens. She loved the house, but was forced to sign over the estate to the Exchequer when her husband William was discovered to have defrauded £80,000 from the Treasury. The estate is now used as the headquarters of the Scout Association while the house is a hotel and conference centre.

Bruce Castle,
Lordship Lane, Tottenham

Three-quarters of a mile south of the Enfield border, Bruce Castle is actually a Tudor mansion that was known as Tottenham Manor house until it was renamed by Henry, 2nd Lord Coleraine in the seventeenth century. It is now a museum.

It is said that Henry imprisoned his beautiful first wife Constantia in a small chamber in the clock tower above the entrance porch, but on 3 November 1680 she climbed out of the window and threw herself to her death, with her infant son in her arms. She has reappeared and her final anguished screams have been heard many times since, always on 3 November. In the early twentieth century, a priest held a service in the chamber and her screams seemed to stop – although in 1996 some people in Bruce Castle Park believed that they heard Constantia's screams, and her ghost continues to occasionally be seen to fall silently from the window.

Another apparition takes the form of a ghostly group of people in eighteenth-century costume who were seen outside the house on two separate occasions late at night in 1971. They appeared to be dancing but did so in complete silence and were seen to fade away.

Former STC Factory,
New Southgate

The former Standard Telephones & Cables (STC) factory complex is now the North London Business Park. In its heyday STC was one of the largest employers in North London and owned the site from 1922 until 1991, when the company was taken over by Northern Telecom (later Nortel) who shut down the site eleven years later.

Only one of the original buildings from the 1920s still stands, and it was rumoured amongst STC staff to be haunted by a tall, hooded monk. For some, the apparition was more than a rumour. He was seen by a security guard, who was so shaken that he refused to do any more night patrols in that building. Some years ago, I spoke to one of the cleaners, who saw the monk during a violent thunderstorm.

The factory was built on land that had been part of the Great Northern Cemetery, and a chapel and mortuary had stood where the factory building was later built. These were built in the nineteenth century to serve the cemetery, but if the apparition is that of a monk, it may date back to a much earlier time, when the land was owned by the Abbots of St Albans.

Oak Hill Park, East Barnet

Oak Hill Park follows the course of Pymme's Brook as it flows through East Barnet on its way towards Edmonton and beyond. A number of apparitions have been seen wandering through the park at night. One evening in the 1950s, two girls were walking through the park when they saw a man dressed in old-fashioned clothes sitting on a bench. As they got nearer to the man he disappeared in an instant, and in the early hours of Christmas morning 1958 a man and his girlfriend heard the sound of a horse galloping towards them. The sound grew louder and louder as though the horse was getting closer, although they couldn't see any horses. When it sounded as though the horse was almost upon them they heard a loud neigh and the unseen horse seemed to change direction and galloped away. Was this a psychic echo of the aftermath of the Battle of Barnet, as discussed in chapter three?

BIBLIOGRAPHY

Allemandy, Victor H., *Enfield Past & Present* (Meyers, Brooks & Co., 1914)

Boudier, Gary, *A-Z of Enfield's Pubs Part 1* (Gary Boudier 2000)

Boudier, Gary, *A-Z of Enfield's Pubs Part 2* (Gary Boudier 2002)

Burne, Alfred, *The Battlefields of England* (Methuen, 1950)

Campbell, Patrick, *Trent Park: A History* (Middlesex University Press, 1997)

Carter, Valerie (ed.), *Treasures of Enfield* (Enfield Preservation Society, 2000)

Celoria, F. (ed.), *London Studies: Topography, Archaeology, Folklife, No. 1* (1974)

Cobban, Jennie Lee, *Geoffrey de Mandeville and London's Camelot* (Jennie Lee Cobban, 1997)

Cresswell, Henrietta, *Winchmore Hill: Memories of a Lost Village* (Southgate Civic Trust, 1982)

Delvin, S. A., *History of Winchmore Hill* (Regency Press, 1987)

Edwards, Jack, *Cheshunt in Hertfordshire* (Cheshunt Urban District Council, 1974)

Edwards, Jack, *The Story of Capel* (Jack Edwards, 1985)

Forman, Joan, *The Haunted South* (Robert Hale Ltd, 1978)

Gillam, Geoffrey, *Theatres, Music Halls & Cinemas in the London Borough of Enfield* (Enfield Archaeological Society, 1986)

Gillam, Geoffrey, *Forty Hall, Enfield, 1629-1997* (Enfield Archaeological Society, 1997)

Herbert, E. H., *Ghost Trains*

Ingram, John H., *Haunted Homes & Family Legends of Great Britain* (Reeves & Turner, 1912)

Jones, Richard, *Walking Haunted London* (New Holland, 1999)

O'Donnell, Elliott, *Ghosts of London* (Philip Allan, 1932)

Pam, David, *Southgate and Winchmore Hill – a Short History* (G. J. Lawrence, 1982)

Pam, David, *The Story of Enfield Chase* (Enfield Preservation Society, 1984)

Pam, David, *A Parish Near London* (Enfield Preservation Society, 1990)

Pam, David, *A Victorian Suburb* (Enfield Preservation Society, 1992)

Playfair, Guy Lyon, *This House is Haunted* (Souvenir Press, 1980)

Spencer, John & Anne, *The Poltergeist Phenomenon* (Headline, 1997)

Spencer, John & Anne, *The Encyclopedia of Ghosts and Spirits, Volume 2* (Headline, 2001)

Websites

www.booksie.com/memoir/book/martin_harrow/dont-play-with-the-harrow-kids

www.capelmanorgardens.co.uk

www.enfarchsoc.org

www.enfieldsociety.org.uk

www.farsightfiles.co.uk/2009/03/21/enfield-royal-british-legion-isp-investigation-2

www.fortyhallestate.co.uk

www.nlpi.co.uk

www.trentparkopenhouse.com

www.visitleevalley.org.uk/en/content/cms/nature/gardens-heritage/myddelton-house-gardens